# WAR AT SEA

## Canada and the Battle of the Atlantic

## KEN SMITH

NIMBUS
PUBLISHING

NIMBUS.CA

Nimbus Publishing Limited
3731 Mackintosh St, Halifax, NS B3K 5A5
(902) 455-4286 nimbus.ca

Printed and bound in Canada
NB1152

Design: John van der Woude Designs

Library and Archives Canada Cataloguing in Publication

Smith, Ken, 1949 September 16-, author
War at sea : Canada and the battle of the Atlantic / Ken Smith.
Includes bibliographical references.
Issued in print and electronic formats.
ISBN 978-1-77108-265-5 (pbk.).—ISBN 978-1-77108-266-2 (html)

1. World War, 1939-1945—Naval operations, Canadian. 2. World War, 1939-1945—Campaigns—Atlantic Ocean. 3. Canada—Armed Forces— History—World War, 1939-1945. I. Title.

D779.C2S65 2015    940.54'5971    C2015-900247-8
C2015-900248-6

Nimbus Publishing acknowledges the financial support for its publishing activities from the Government of Canada through the Canada Book Fund (CBF) and the Canada Council for the Arts, and from the Province of Nova Scotia through Film & Creative Industries Nova Scotia. We are pleased to work in partnership with Film & Creative Industries Nova Scotia to develop and promote our creative industries for the benefit of all Nova Scotians.

*This book is dedicated to all those young men and women who, in the face of extreme odds, fought with grim perseverance and total dedication against a stealthy, unseen enemy in an often unforgiving sea.*

# CONTENTS

# INTRODUCTION

O N September 3rd, 1939, Great Britain declared war on Germany, following a blitzkrieg attack on Poland by forces of the Adolf Hitler–led Third Reich. Over the next five years, total war, global in scope and brutal in its intensity, consumed much of our civilized world. By the time the conflict was over, the destruction and sheer carnage on both the Allied and Axis sides were virtually incalculable.

Germany had prepared well. Despite the harsh restrictions laid down by the Treaty of Versailles, Hitler had, in a mere dozen years, through political manipulation, lies, false promises, and downright threats, brought Germany from a thoroughly beaten post–First World War state to one of the world's leading economies backed by the most powerful military force in the world. Hitler sought world domination and was ready to carry out his master plan, diabolical as it was.

The German naval forces, utilizing their highly competent submarine fleet of Unterseebootes—U-boats—would quickly become the scourge of the high seas, seeking out the main shipping lanes for their attacks on British merchantmen. England had quickly realized it would need an unlimited amount of troops, war material, and supplies if it were to survive the German threat. Britain's import lifeline included wheat, rubber, oil, weapons, troops, ammunition, and raw materials shipped from all corners of its vast empire. Cutting these British trade routes was vital to German success, and the Mediterranean Sea, the Caribbean, the Indian Ocean, and virtually anywhere ships bound for England could be found and waylaid were targeted. This, of course, included the North Atlantic, reaching west as far as Canadian and US coastal waters.

When war broke out, Britain was ill-prepared on land or in air. At sea, the Royal Navy (RN) was still considered the world's largest and was much stronger than the German naval forces in terms of numbers of large surface ships. But Britain also recognized that, since the Commonwealth must be protected, the available seagoing warships would be spread quite thin. The Germans, however reticent to use their surface fleet, still had a large and growing U-boat fleet numbering 57 vessels, and although only a few dozen were available for immediate sea duty, many more were nearing completion. (By 1945, 463 were on patrol.) Rear Admiral Karl Doenitz, appointed overall Commander of Germany's submarine fleet in 1939, was convinced that, if given 300 U-boats, he could bring Britain to its knees economically. Doenitz's confident plea caught the ear of Hitler, who agreed. As it turned out, it wasn't quite so simple, as only by 1943 did Doenitz reach his stated allotment of 300 U-boats. Yet it was not without reason that Britain's great war leader, Winston Churchill, later said of the German Kriegsmarine, "The only thing that ever really frightened me during the war was the U-boat peril."

Initially, Britain was not overly concerned by Germany's sea power, assuming England's great naval presence, consisting mostly of huge, sleek battleships, cruisers, and destroyers, would be sufficient to deter any serious shipping attacks. Despite the huge amount of shipping losses inflicted on Britain in the First World War, the British Admiralty felt that they had a powerful enough surface fleet, and that, combined with advances in ASDIC (sonar) and radar technology, it would be sufficient to keep the Germans at bay. The competence of the German U-boat commanders dispelled within months the notion that the war at sea would easily go in Britain's favour.

The British Admiralty had also expected the Germans to play the naval war using agreed-upon rules of honour. They soon learned otherwise. The Germans, using Goering's vaunted air power in support of the U-boats, were soon running up high tonnage rates, that is, sinking many tons of cargo carried by merchant ships trying to get safely to British ports in one piece. Britain, in 1939, undertook a huge shipbuilding program as the military realized many new ships were needed, especially those of the destroyer, frigate, and corvette classes. In the interim, Britain fought back hard, holding its own but desperately needing more ships to protect territories in the Mediterranean, the Caribbean, India, and Canada.

Within hours of Britain's declaration of war, German U-boats, thinking it was a merchant carrier, sunk the American liner *Athenia* with the loss of 118 people. Nazi leader Adolph Hitler was incensed as the attack went against his orders. For a short period, Hitler scaled back his attacks, fearing they might draw the US into the conflict, something he was not yet ready to face. However, British ships were still being picked off by lone U-boats roaming the waters off England and France.

By the end of 1939, only a few months into the war, Britain realized the war at sea would not be fought against surface ships, but against Germany's U-boats. Although surface ships did do considerable damage to merchant shipping in the first year of the war at sea, the U-boats were most successful, whether through chance encounters with British ships or in daring raids on English naval strongholds, such as Commander Gunther Prien's U-47 attack at Scapa Flow, where he sunk the HMS *Royal Oak* at anchor in Scapa Bay.

In a very short time, utilizing a new and highly effective tactic involving U-boat wolfpacks, the Germans would inflict much more serious damage. By the end of 1940, France, the Low Countries, and Norway had fallen to the German might. The war at sea was about to change radically as the Kriegsmarine took over vital French ports including the shipyards at Brest, Lorient, St. Nazaire, and Ostend. U-boats could now reach far into the Atlantic with the support of air cover. The mid-ocean refuelling this development also allowed for meant U-boats could now reach Canadian and American coastlines.

Allied air support could not yet reach the midpoint of the Atlantic Ocean, thus leaving convoys without much-needed cover. This area was called the "Black Hole," and it was here that hundreds of merchant ships were lost to enemy torpedoes. The period between mid-1940 and early 1941 was known by German U-boat crews as the "happy times," as Allied shipping losses were in the millions of tons with over three hundred merchant ships being sunk. Between January and July 1942, four hundred Allied merchant ships were lost and only seven U-boats sunk.

Eventually the Battle of the Atlantic would become the longest single engagement of the Second World War. Although the Germans continued to have U-boats at their disposal, a combination of Allied ships, long-range planes, improved radar, sonar, radio, and effective search-and-destroy tactics successfully harassed the U-boat fleet to the point that their missions and encounters became almost suicidal. Out of a total of approximately forty thousand U-boat crew members, over thirty thousand perished. By 1944, German subs were no longer considered a major convoy threat, but that is not to say the danger had completely disappeared. Vigilance was still a top priority, even up to the last day of the war.

AT THE OUTSET OF THE SECOND WORLD WAR, THE Canadian navy consisted of only thirty-five hundred personnel, and a fleet of six destroyers and a mere thirteen vessels. Dependence on the powerful British Navy had given Canada a sense of security, but now it was time for action. A difficult task lay ahead, and within months a massive shipbuilding program was underway.

Canadian shipyards were filling orders for sixty-four Flower Class corvettes and twenty-eight Bangor Class minesweepers. Production abilities were limited to building these smaller ships as the Canadian shipyards were not yet equipped or designed to build the much heavier and more sophisticated warships. And these smaller ships were built to suit Canada's needs, which were to protect the country's home ports, monitor approaches, lay defensive mine patterns, and provide escort to merchant ships. This sufficed for the first year of the conflict, until events in Europe in 1940 convinced Canada to embark on a much larger corvette and minesweeper-building program.

By the end of the conflict, the RCN grew to over 350 vessels, including 17 destroyers, 2 cruisers, 68 frigates, 112 corvettes, 67 minesweepers, 12 escort ships, 9 motor torpedo boats, 75 fairmile motor launches, 12 armoured yachts, and several vessels of other types. As well, by 1945 the RCN's naval ranks would number nearly 100,000. As a result, Canada's navy would, in five years, rise to become the third-largest in the world. But it was never easy, especially in the early years when the young sailors, often under-trained and worked to exhaustion on poorly equipped ships, found the agony of freezing to death in a frigid open sea never far from their thoughts.

The number of young men signing up with the navy was quite plentiful in 1939, so initially care was taken in the recruitment process to find as many experienced men as possible in the Royal Canadian Naval Reserve. But, by 1940, with so many ships being turned out, it had become impossible to fill all crew positions. There just weren't enough experienced men available. As a result, the volunteer reserve was created and used as a pool from which inexperienced men were drawn. Until these new men were sufficiently trained on all aspects of their assigned duties, they and their ships were in great peril. But the great majority of the young men who signed up proved to be willing. Many rose to leadership ranks.

Basic training was minimal and many training officers were themselves without sailing experience. Signalling methods, weapons training, and detection skills would, for some, come only with actual enemy encounters, often much too late. Many of the new recruits who trained in under-equipped and understaffed local naval divisions received their baptism of fire not in Canadian waters, but off the shores of England, Iceland, Norway, and France, where they were initially sent to help deter marauding U-boats. But despite the harshest of conditions, the new recruits and young officers of the growing RCN fleet grew in their assigned roles, warranting recognition as a valid fighting assemblage of their own, not to be shackled by British command but to fight as a true Canadian naval unit. Slowly, as experience rose and the number of ships (and support airplanes) grew, the RCN would prove itself.

Canada's scanty initial allotment of ships was assigned to convoy escort duties, mine laying, port patrols, and submarine detection. The challenge at hand would not be easy; all duties had inherent dangers. U-boats, by 1940, were not operating as yet in the far western Atlantic, and convoys were able to make it to the midpoint of the Atlantic crossing where they would be picked up by an escort of destroyers to complete the convoy crossing to Britain. By the end of 1940, the RCN had not as yet lost a ship to enemy action, although three Canadian vessels had been destroyed through collision, sea conditions, or fire, resulting in the loss of hundreds of men.

By 1941, both Germans and Allies knew that the struggle for control of the sea lanes would be fought between submarines and small-but-nimble corvettes and frigates, as well as fast, weapon-laden destroyers. In the same year, over sixty corvettes were built and ready for duty, with scores of

*Burial at sea of Ordinary Seaman Kenneth Watson of the RCN destroyer* HMCS Assiniboine. *Seaman Watson was mortally injured during the sinking of a U-boat on August 6, 1942.* (Library and Archives Canada PA-115346)

warships, including frigates, minesweepers, and motor patrol boats, eagerly anticipated but on the way. A robust recruitment program expanded the RCN's enrolment to ten thousand within the same period, increasing the navy's strength five-fold, the highest of all the Allied navies. In the haste to get the warships prepared for active service, many were not yet completely fitted with proper radar, ASDIC, or deck guns, and had to sail to England to complete fitting at experienced dockyards. In one case with an incomplete corvette, an interim log was inserted to simulate where the forward four-inch gun was to be installed.

New or improved weapon and detection technology was still mostly being designed, and training at most times was difficult, hurried, and too fundamental, with seasickness rampant. Impatient commanders had to show much forbearance, and ships' officers were often a harried lot, trying to impart knowledge on their young charges while at the same time going about their own duties. Warships, especially corvettes, were wet, uncomfortable, and usually overcrowded with new recruits and regular crew members, and the Atlantic, volatile at the best of times, did not make training conditions easier. Tasks could be learned, but mastering them took time.

Reliable ASDIC operators, perhaps the most vital asset to a warship and its crew, were at a premium until well into the conflict, and the waters of Atlantic Canada made sonar operations extremely unreliable. The British may have been proud of their radar, but far too many RCN warships lacked this equipment. This shortage, combined with the German U-boat tactics of "hunting" on the surface at night, made the subs virtually undetectable, as the British ASDIC sonar system would only be effective on a submerged sub.

Initially German subs did not target the small St. Lawrence sector, but as opportunities presented themselves, including the shortage of RCN escort ships, the number of attacks mounted. Unfortunately the worst was yet to come, as the U-boats, now hunting in dreaded wolfpacks, sought new targets within sight of Canadian soil. Merchant ships in 1941 sailed only in protective convoys and in designated areas. Escort forces were established, covering principal convoy routes from Quebec City, Quebec; Halifax, Nova Scotia; Sydney, Nova Scotia; St. John's, Newfoundland; and Iceland. But with the Germans in France, RCN warships were reassigned to British waters, leaving Canada virtually helpless should major attacks occur near its own ports. By the spring of 1942, this lack of proper protection, along with the ill-equipped ships available, would prove to be disastrous to merchant and RCN warships alike, as the lethal U-boats sought fresh targets in Canadian waters.

In the early years of the war, the German Kriegsmarine was quick to scoff and publicly deride the RCN as being weak and ineffectual. But eventually, by sheer numbers of warships, improved radar, ASDIC technology, and superior coordinated air support, the RCN evolved into a massive and potent naval fighting force, becoming a major asset in the defeat of the German Kriegsmarine.

THIS BOOK FOCUSES ON THE BATTLE OF THE ATLANTIC, a bitter and costly affair in which 2,000 members of the RCN were lost in the struggle to rid the area of the U-boat threat. More specifically, emphasis will be placed on the defence of Canadian waters surrounding the Atlantic provinces, including the Gulf of St. Lawrence, in which 23 of the 58 Canadian registered merchant vessels, as well as 4 RCN warships, were lost to German submarine attacks between 1942 and 1945. In this secondary conflict 372 Allied persons lost their lives.

It was to be a long, hard struggle with both sides suffering agonizing losses and bittersweet victories. Not all confrontations occurred at sea. There were Nazi spies who landed in Canada, prison camp breakouts, U-boats that fired at shore, and in one case, a number of armed Germans actually came ashore to set up a radar station.

A chapter offering brief descriptions of the various types of Canadian warships, as well as the weaponry used, is included. *War at Sea* also offers a profile of U-boats and their potent firepower and resolute commanders. Throughout the book are accounts, often harrowing and dramatic, in the words of veterans themselves, who felt that their stories must be told as a way of passing the flame of remembrance to younger generations.

### A Cook's Life

*I liked to cook. I made good pastry. My pies were good, without bragging. I learned from a good man. His name was Norman Dodds. He was my first officer and he wouldn't let me go to sea. He kept in Admiralty House for about four years. I skipped basic training. Can't be spared, can't be spared. Old Norm, he had friends in high places and can't spare him, can't spare him. I guess I was indispensable, and didn't know it. My galley wasn't half the size of this room. I could touch all four walls standing in the centre. I was an officers' cook and then everything changed. It went permanent ship's company, everybody ate alike. We had a soup or juice, a main course, a potato, two vegetables, a dessert and a savoury, which was a cheese dish. Savoury dish was just like toast with cheese and a bit of bacon chopped in it, whatever. As long as it had cheese in it, it was called a savoury. The airmen, they were ill fed, we might say. And they didn't have as good cooks as the Canadian navy did. And if we came alongside, they used to come over for a good meal because, well, not bragging, but we were better cooks because we had the quality food. I said it was quality food made us better cooks.*

*We were back aft and the stern of the ship used to wave like a tail up and down, flip flop. I never lost too many meals, but it was too rough; and I used to go forward to the main galley and get enough to feed, I fed 12 officers. And this one time when I was coming back, a wave come across the midships and that food is still going, I was still holding on. I never let anybody know I couldn't swim. I used to get somebody to take my tests for me. I cheated. I like rum and coke, well mixed. I could never take it straight. Some could take theirs, throw*

*Petty Officer Cook Bert Grant preparing Christmas pudding aboard the* HMCS Stadacona, *Nova Scotia, December 1941. A well-fed ship was a happy ship, but when action stations sounded, the cook would rush to his assigned battle task—perhaps helping a gunner, or even manning a pompom, Bofors, or Oerlikon cannon.* (Library and Archives Canada PA-105652)

*it back. I could not do that. I had to, I was a sissy when it comes to that; I had it well mixed with coke. I didn't drink all my rum. I saved it in a bottle, which was against the rules. I used to take it home and enjoy it at home. Two and half ounces in a cup or a glass, whatever you took up, the coxswain used to pour it in and over your glass; and he always give you overflow, it was called spillers. You got more than two and a half ounces. As a petty officer, I didn't have to drink it there. I could drink it in my mess. Seamen used to have to take a drink, God bless her, the Queen, God bless her, and down it. Tear the throat out of you.*

—William White, Halifax, Nova Scotia, courtesy
The Historica Memory Project

### *At Least a Stoker is Warm!*

*After getting out and seeing the Atlantic in the winter, I was glad to be a stoker. I was down below deck where it was warm and I thought, if we get torpedoed by a submarine, I want to be gone quick because my abandon ship station was a carley float and it wouldn't have lasted ten minutes in the North Atlantic, you would have frozen to death.*

*I was in the stoke hold, and you were down there all alone because you had two different stoke holds to look after, an Action Station bell went, well, I'd be there until the all clear went. If I wasn't on watch, then everybody had a place they had to go and mine was on the starboard side depth charge store. And I'd be there until we got the all clear. We'd be throwing charges.*

*Every time you were at action stations in a sense you were in danger, and the most dangerous times at sea was*

*Leading Stoker Henri Leclair,* HMCS Assiniboine, *November* 1940. *Though away from the bitter cold and extreme sailing conditions, the stoker's work area was often a prime target for torpedoes, with low survival rates.* (Library and Archives Canada PA-104189)

on moonlight clear nights because a submarine could be on a horizon and still see you. So the best nights we had was when it was real stormy and dark, you felt the safest. And you worried about somebody going on deck and lighting a cigarette because that could be seen for miles.

When we would pick up survivors, sometimes off a trawler or anything that got sunk in the convoy, and bring them onboard, when we could do that safely, like, we were not allowed to stop while we were at action stations, many, many faces would go floating by lost the sea. But when we get an all clear and we could see people around in little sea boats or anything, we'd pick them up and when we brought them back to harbour, they wouldn't go below deck until they got back on land. They had enough of it.

Ice, when you were off watch, you were on deck chipping ice because we'd be top heavy if we didn't. It was survival. Everybody had their turn too. Once you seen the ice, you had to start chipping, get it off because it would make you top heavy. The corvettes didn't cut through the water, they went up and over it and down it. If you went on the toilets, we called it the can, if the ship went up in the air, all the water, little bit of water that was in there would be sucked out. Now the ship sinks down and you get a bath because the water pops up and floods you. It wasn't funny.

The Royal Canadian Navy has a lot to be proud of with what went on during the war because in the end, they were getting all the convoys across and wound up being the third largest navy in the world at that time. We took over the British Navy, they quit the convoy business and so did the Americans. So we were doing it all.

—Robert Hugh Gilmore, Welland, Ontario

# CHAPTER ONE

# SHIPS AND WEAPONS OF THE RCN

B Y 1945, THE RCN HAD UP TO THREE HUNDRED WAR-ships at its disposal, a far cry from the meagre thirteen available in 1939. At the beginning of the war, only a modest naval buildup was undertaken, enough to fulfill the needs for the protection of ports and ships along the Canadian coastline and eastern seaboard. The RCN, by 1941, badly needed larger ships with anti-submarine capabilities, but they were not available yet. In the interim, warships, cheaply built and of various size and design, were rushed to completion at shipyards in eastern and western Canada. The RCN needed, for their immediate purposes, smaller, cheaply built ships which the Canadian shipyards, with their limited capabilities, could produce. Light escort duties as well as patrolling ports, harbour entrances, narrow channels, and areas where lurking U-boats might be found were the anticipated usages for the order which the Canadian government put forth in 1941. Included were sixty-four corvettes and twenty-eight Bangor

Class minesweepers. Much greater pressure was put on the Canadian and British shipyards when France fell to Germany, giving its ships and planes opportunities to reach far into the Allies' Atlantic shipping lanes, wreaking havoc while now using the tactic of hunting in wolfpacks.

# THE SHIPS OF THE RCN

## The Flower Class Corvette

THE CORVETTE WAS BORNE OUT OF NECESSITY AT THE beginning of the Second World War. The Royal Canadian Navy, long dependent on Great Britain's Royal Navy (RN), had originally planned to build its own naval fleet with destroyers and larger ships, but it quickly became apparent that smaller ships were needed as patrol vessels to protect major Atlantic ports and naval facilities, and to allow merchant shipping traffic sufficient convoy protection. It was imperative that some sort of small, speedy vessel with anti-sub competency be built and put into use as soon as possible. Corvettes were only intended for use until the larger and better-equipped destroyers and frigates were made available from the British shipyards. In fact the original intention was to supply the RN with the first ten corvettes built in return for two British-built destroyers, but these plans were cancelled.

British shipbuilders at the Smith's Dock Company came up with a design based on a successful whaling ship which could be constructed cheaply in Canada. Thus the corvette was born, untested and unaware that the outcome of the U-boat challenge in the Battle of the Atlantic would rest heavily on its performance. Approximately half of the first order of corvettes produced were used as convoy escorts and over twenty of these workhorses were lost to German subs, but by the end of the war they had effectively proved their worth time and time again.

The name corvette, given to the short, wide-beamed ship by Winston Churchill after a small sailing ship of old, was deemed superior to the original name, the Patrol Whale-Catcher. Both the RN and RCN had ships in production by 1939, albeit with slightly different designs. With a length of 205 feet and a 33-foot beam, the small ship was relatively slow at 16 knots, but could turn inside any other ship available. With moderate firepower, including a 4-inch bow gun, 2 pom-pom guns, several Lewis machine guns, depth charges, and, later, Hedgehog equipment, the corvette proved

*The corvette HMCS* Moosejaw, *commissioned in June 1941, is credited, along with the HMCS* Chambly, *with having sunk* U-501, *the first recorded U-boat "kill" of the war.* (Library and Archives Canada PA-105829)

able to tackle the roughest seas. But, as expected, there were shortcomings. They were considered "wet ships," their decks often awash with water as they rolled, bucked, swerved, and veered violently, with even hardened sailors becoming seasick at times. But they challenged the slightly faster U-boats in the worst weather the Atlantic could offer. The seamen persevered despite miserable living conditions aboard ship

*The corvette* HMCS Trillium *fights heavy seas, its decks awash. Although corvettes were considered "wet" ships, they would tackle weather even destroyers avoided.* (Library and Archives Canada PA-037474)

and a lack of experience, reliable equipment, and even good leadership. Eventually the crew, most of whom were young men in their early twenties, became outstanding seaman, proud of their successes and determined to finally rid the waters of their homeland from the silent killers always lurking just below the surface.

The largest class of corvettes used by the RCN was the Flower Class, with each ship named after a specific flower; shortly, names of Canadian towns were also included. By 1941, several hundred corvettes were ready for use, most of these destined for use by the RN. A more sophisticated version of the corvette was introduced in 1943, as the Flower Class models were best suited for coastal and river work. The Canadian shipyards were not yet equipped to produce frigates, but the Castle Class corvette, slightly larger and faster than the Flower Class, would serve until frigates were available.

The first few years of the war kept the corvettes on constant convoy duty in various sectors, from Atlantic Canada eastward to the British Isles. In 1942, German subs concentrated on the Gulf of St. Lawrence shipping lanes, causing all sorts of havoc among the merchant carriers streaming from the ports of Montreal and Quebec City. Too few corvettes and frigates were assigned to this large sector, and as a result a score of merchant carriers were lost to German torpedoes. The Canadian government decided to close the St. Lawrence to merchant shipping in 1942, which was a welcome relief to German U-boats which were, more and more, facing constant harassment from corvettes, destroyers, and frigates. Eventually the U-boats exited the area seeking pickings elsewhere, notably off the New England coast.

The early corvettes also had detection-equipment inadequacies. The ASDIC setups were outdated and far from reliable. Eventually the corvettes would be fitted with upgraded and more reliable detection technology. However, communication with merchant ships in convoy was difficult and almost impossible at night, and miscommunication resulted in many lives lost. Despite the frustrations in seeing merchant carriers in their charge sunk before their very eyes, as well as other ships carrying their comrades, the RCN grew, working in unison with the RCAF patrols. Just as the Spitfire was so instrumental in the Battle of Britain, so too was this unheralded, short, wide-beamed ship.

### Cook to Gunner Helper—in 60 Seconds!

*I was cook, I started as galley boy and worked myself up of course to assistant cook, then second cook and eventually became a chief cook. Well, it was very interesting, but in them days, a lot of powdered eggs and dried potatoes and powdered milk of course. And in England, your stores weren't very good because we only bought them the same thing, so we had good food when we were in Canada or sailed out of Canadian or American ports.*

*The greatest part I found myself was just waiting for them to hit the button for, you know, action stations. But once you got into action stations, like the man said, you know, you didn't have time to look. You went up there, especially for aircraft at us. I was on the, what you call Oerlikons. They're anti-aircraft guns and we had a five millimetre Oerlikon gun. And my job was to put these shells in these cans and then hand it to the DEMS gunner, DEMS stand for Defend Every Merchant Ship [Defensively Equipped Merchant Ship].*

*And he would handle the gun, but merchant seamen themselves didn't have too much experience on the guns, although we did take the guns at times. And I can remember one time, I was with an inexperienced DEMS gunner and the minute the aircraft come over the horizon, he started firing away and I said, "For God's sakes, man, you wait until he comes into your sights," I said, "and let go then." I said, "I can't feed these cans as fast as you're shooting them off." I can remember that incident. I think I was on* Hillcrest Park *at the time.*

*But we were great buddies aboard ship. Everybody looked for everybody else. If you forgot your life jacket, there was always somebody there to make sure he ran for your life jacket in the galley or in your cabin, wherever you happened to have it. And he would always be watching your back.*

*—Gilles Doucet, Bathurst, New Brunswick*

## The River Class Frigate

WHILE THE FLOWER CLASS corvettes were doing the best they could, the RCN was in desperate need of a larger ship designed specifically for long-range transatlantic convoy duty. This meant a vessel not only larger than the diminutive corvettes, but something which could reach at least 20 knots on the open sea with medium range distance capabilities of at least 11,000 kilometres. The ship would also need endurance and sufficient weaponry to enable it to engage successfully in anti-submarine warfare. State-of-the-art systems of detection, radar, radio, and ASDIC surveillance would be imperative with well-trained crews and an officer complement of 145. Designed by British naval engineer William Read, the first of 151 River Class frigates, as they were to be called, was launched in Britain in 1941 at the Smith's Dock Company at Southbank-on-Tees. Built in both British and Canadian shipyards at very reasonable cost, the ships.were, at 86.3 metres and with a beam of 11.1 metres, a somewhat larger version of a corvette, but smaller and less sophisticated than a destroyer. Reciprocating steam engines powering twin screws were used rather than the turbines used on the slower corvettes, although building processes pioneered on corvette construction were also used on the frigates.

The frigates were much better armed than the corvettes, with twin four-inch guns on the foredeck and a twelve-pound gun on aft, with depth charges and mortars. The frigates also had the latest in accurate anti-sub Hedgehog firing technology and advanced detection technology as it became available.

The first frigate commissioned in Canada was the *Waskesui*, launched in June 1943. As good as these new frigates were, most of them entered the war only after the German subs were already being harassed, so the bulk of the accolades went to the smaller corvettes. But the frigates still had work to do, and they did it well. Of the twenty-nine German U-boats sunk by Canadian ships, no less than twelve were lost to frigates. Canada's top "ace," with four kills, was the frigate HMCS *Swansea*. After the war, many of the frigates were stripped down and scrapped, or sunk and used as breakwaters. Over twenty were eventually renovated and refitted to become ships of the Prestonian Class, to be used for training. One frigate did become quite famous when Greek shipping magnate Aristotle Onassis purchased the HMCS *Stormont* and turned it into his privately owned luxury yacht, *Christina O*.

## The Minesweeper

THE CANADIAN PORTS OF HALIFAX, ST. JOHN'S, SYDNEY, Quebec City, and several others were kept busy with convoy traffic throughout the war. Supply lines simply had to be kept open. The Allies had assumed at the outset that Germany, with its powerful submarine fleet, would focus on placing mines in all major ports, harbours, narrows, and congested enemy points of passage. In 1939, Canada's minesweeper strength consisted of four ships, hardly enough to cover the expected threat. So, as with the case of the corvettes and frigates, orders were authorized for the quick construction of these small-beamed ships. Also like the frigates and corvettes, minesweepers were much smaller than destroyers and cruisers, and a lot less sophisticated, enabling Canadian shipyards to build them.

The Bangor Class sweepers each displaced 672 tons with a length of 54.9 metres and a width of 8.7 metres. Crewed with a complement of 83 men, the Bangors were capable of running at 16 knots. Armed with 40 depth charges, a fore-mounted 12-pounder gun, as well as two 20-millimetre Oerlikon anti-aircraft guns, the Bangors were indeed capable, although quite unstable in rough seas, with many sailors considering them worse than the Flower Class corvettes. But, like their larger cousins, they got the job done. (Later, a larger and improved version of the Bangor minesweeper, called the Algerine Class, was produced, only ten of which served in the RCN, mostly in escort duties.)

Eventually fifty-four Bangor Class minesweepers would be built, but the German mine-laying agenda wasn't as extensive as expected. In fact, German mines were only laid once in Canadian waters, so many of these ships were equipped and put to use in patrol duties and as convoy escorts in the Gulf of St. Lawrence and other sections along the Atlantic coast. They were, however, used extensively as minesweepers during Operation Neptune (D-Day) in the English Channel. In fact, of the sixteen minesweepers sent to help in Operation Neptune, only one ship had actual experience in mine-laying operations, but they did all undergo extensive training in England prior to the invasion. The British commanders initially had misgivings as to whether or not the Canadian sailors would be up to the task of minesweeping properly, but after several rugged training exercises the senior British naval officers were quick to admit that the RCN crews were "keen, efficient, and competent."

The Germans used mainly contact mines and later magnetic and acoustic types. But the Canadian-built minesweepers were effective in cutting the mine anchor cables, changing magnetic current strengths to nullify magnetic mines, or creating sound enhancers to throw off acoustic-triggered devices.

Five RCN minesweepers were lost in the Second World War.

## Destroyers

AT THE OUTSET OF THE SECOND WORLD WAR, THE RCN had a meagre six destroyers, built by the RN in the early 1930s. Eight more River Class destroyers were received from the RN between 1939 and 1944. As well, the US Navy gave six aging Town Class destroyers to the RCN. With the addition of four Tribal Class destroyers built in Britain, the RCN fleet grew considerably between 1942 and 1944. Used primarily as mid-ocean convoy escorts, five of the RCN's River Class destroyers were lost or heavily damaged during the Battle of the Atlantic.

River Class destroyers had a complement of 181 all ratings, displaced over 1,300 tons, and were 90 metres in length with a beam of 10.1 metres. They were able to cruise at substantial speeds, easily covering an ocean span. Torpedoes, mortars, depth charges, four 120-millimetre guns, two 12.7-millimetre guns, and six 20-millimetre Oerlikon flak guns were included in the arsenal and all destroyers were equipped with the most

*The foredeck of* HMCS *Prince Henry. Originally a Canadian passenger liner converted to an armed merchant cruiser, the* Prince Henry *survived the war, taking part in several key operations and patrols.* (Library and Archives Canada E002852526)

*Two unidentified men in the control room of a ship; from the size, possibly a destroyer.* (Library and Archives Canada PA-213206)

up-to-date anti-submarine detection devices, including ASDIC, HF/DF, radar, and, while it was available, the all-important Enigma decoding device.

## Motor Torpedo Boats

THESE LITTLE BOATS, LIGHT AND POCKET-SIZED, WERE designed for fast strikes and quick getaways. At 21 metres in length, the RCN motor torpedo boats (MTBs) were armed with 6-pounder guns, .303- or .50-calibre machine guns, and either 40-millimetre Bofors or 20-millimetre Oerlikon guns. These speedy little devils could do over 40 knots and were prepared to do a lot of damage with two 21-inch torpedo tubes, as well as depth charge launchers. With three shafts, each powered by Rolls Royce supercharged V-12 engines kicking 3,750 horsepower, the MTBs could range up to 260 kilometres in the course of a single patrol.

Used primarily for coastal defences and hit-and-run raids, usually at night, these pint-sized boats were also effective for low speed ambush as they were highly manoeuvrable, produced little wake, and minimal sound. Their job, to disrupt enemy traffic and shipping, was difficult, especially in rough seas, and they were never far away from enemy attack from sea or air. The crews of these boats did long patrols and saw plenty of action. Besides coastal duty, MTBs were used extensively at the Dunkirk evacuation, the St. Nazaire raid, as well as in Operation Neptune. With barely any armour, the MTBs proved to be a reliable and effective addition to the RCN's growing fleet of ships and boats of every size.

## Fairmile Motor Launch

PERHAPS THE SMALLEST WARSHIP OF THE RCN, THE fairmile launch was used extensively by coastal forces in anti-submarine patrols, port defence, and rescue duties in the Gulf of St. Lawrence. The launches were originally intended as a stopgap measure until larger ships were available for duty in Atlantic Canada. Somewhat shorter than the MTBs and propelled by two 630-horsepower gas engines, the light, wooden-hulled fairmile could still produce enough speed to run down a U-boat. Besides being outfitted with twenty 300-pound

*Fairmile Q084, May, 1943. These diminutive and speedy little ships are among the unsung heroes in the RCN war at sea. Eighty fairmiles were built in Canada and were involved in port defence, rescue duties, and mine recovery.* (Library and Archives Canada PA-134191)

depth charges, the fairmile also carried a 3-pound gun on the foredeck and machine guns at the aft. Designed by the British Fairmile Company, eighty of the "Little Ships," as they were sometimes referred to, were built in thirteen Canadian shipyards. The fairmiles were known to have excellent sea qualities, but in rough conditions the small ships were tossed around quite severely, and, facing steady drenching sprays, the crews were often less durable than the boats themselves.

Numbered from Q50 to Q129, rather than being given a name like their much larger counterparts, fairmiles were referred to by crews as "Q Ships." At 79 tons, these "little ships" were capable of packing a lethal wallop and served the RCN well.

# WEAPONS AND DETECTION (RCN)

THE FRIGID WATERS OF THE NORTH ATLANTIC, BY LATE 1943, carried hundreds of warships of the Canadian and British navies, all now virtually bristling with weapons at this, the height of the Battle of the Atlantic. Although enemy surface ships were sometimes encountered, the biggest threat still came from the huge U-boat concentration which was constantly on the prowl throughout the Atlantic, seeking fresh kills on a daily basis. A U-boat, as the RCN soon discovered, could not be destroyed easily. Spotting a sub was one thing; chasing it down and destroying it was another, as scores of German U-boats had shown by taking severe hits and still limping away, often after having successfully sunk RCN ships. Torpedoes, of course, were the weapons of choice for German submarines, but how was this countered on the warships of the RCN? What weapons did they use, on what ships, and to what effect?

## The Depth Charge

IF THE TORPEDO WAS THE WEAPON FEARED MOST BY CREWS of RCN ships, then German U-boat crews equally dreaded the depth charge. Taking a well-placed and direct hit often meant oblivion. Depth charges of various design, fitting, and sophistication were carried aboard virtually all ships of the RCN, from battleships to motor launches.

The concept of firing a mine or mortar charge set to explode at a specific depth was first tried in Britain in 1913. By 1916 an effective model, carrying a 140-kilogram charge of TNT or Amatol, loaded in a canister, and pre-set to detonate by hydrostatic pressure at up to 80 feet, was developed. Between wars, the depth charges were much improved in safety, design, and ease of launching. Sinking velocities, detonation charges, and accurate placement were vital considerations as the hulls of German submarines were quite effective in withstanding damage up to almost 5 metres. If the sub had suffered previous damage, it was much more susceptible to a fatal blast. In fact *U-517* survived a severe attack of nearly 700 depth charges thrown at it over a number of hours by two Canadian warships, the *Haida* and the *Iroquois*. Nerve-racking to say the least, but many of the depth charges exploded a safe distance from their target. At first only 2–4 depth charges were carried aboard ships, but this number increased as they became available. By the end of the Second World War, 16,451 of the 74,441 depth charges on hand had been fired.

The earliest method of launching was simply to roll the "ashcans," as they were called by the crews, off the ship. This was considered a dangerous procedure for a slower-moving ship, risking serious damage if the charge went off too close to its own hull. Necessity being the mother of invention, RN engineers designed various launchers, each improving on the last. Mark II and Mark IV depth charge launchers eventually became standard on all RCN ships, with warheads effective up to 150 metres. The Mark VIII, a 21-inch torpedo, was also developed, and by 1944 the RN had fired approximately 3,500 of these. Issued mostly on cruisers and destroyers, the Mark VIII carried a lethal 340-kilogram explosive charge with a range of 4,570 metres at 40 knots. They were also fitted on motor torpedo boats, as well as various torpedo bombers.

The Hedgehog, developed in 1943, was a vast improvement, being able to fire twenty-four depth charges in a set pattern

*The Hedgehog depth charge technology was introduced into RCN service in 1942 and proved to have a higher sinking rate than the standard depth charge. The Hedgehog was fired and detonated in an array pattern, exploding on contact rather than at depth, without affecting ASDIC readings.* (Library and Archives Canada PA-112918)

which detonated only on contact, or on the sea bottom. A big advantage of the Hedgehog was the ships's ability to maintain ASDIC contact throughout an attack, including while firing, though ironically if a U-boat was hit, the ASDIC lost contact. Before the Hedgehog, the ASDIC had to be shut off when launching depth charges. In 1944 the Squid was developed, which could fire three barrelled charges in a triangular pattern, specially designed to crush a submarine's hull.

The use of depth charges and torpedoes was not exclusive to warships as they were also used to good effect by patrol airplanes, especially when taking part in a co-ordinated attack involving ASDIC and radar.

A call to action stations often meant a depth charge attack on an enemy ship, and invariably generated much excitement aboard ship. Both sides jockeyed for attack or escape positions amidst the thunderous explosions, alarms, bells, and shouted orders while the crews of the U-boats could only try and weather the storm. The depth charges proved their lethal value as in more than 100 convoy battles and 1,000 single ship confrontations over 783 U-boats were lost. Conversely, 175 Allied warships and 3,500 merchants ships were damaged or destroyed, the majority as a result of one or more torpedoes.

## Naval Mines

NAVAL MINES USED BY THE RCN IN THE BATTLE OF THE Atlantic were explosive devices designed to blast holes in the hulls of unsuspecting enemy ships of any size, and were powerful enough to cripple or sink even the largest vessel.

Triggered by contact, these stationary mines were used by both the Allied and German naval forces in both defensive and offensive roles. Easily as effective as a torpedo or depth charge when strung out along a narrow passageway such as a harbour entrance, these powerful charges were able to cause serious damage and delays to shipping and sailing schedules, as well as considerable psychological distress. Ships, including submarines, could either lay down mines or drop them into enemy harbours by plane where the mines waited, floating patiently for an unsuspecting ship to trigger what was often a fatal strike.

By late 1939 the RN, having suffered considerable and unacceptable shipping losses, was able to retrieve a German mine intact, and with intensive scrutiny was able to develop effective countermeasures against the always dangerous magnetic and, later, acoustic mines. Larger battleships and troop-carrying vessels were equipped with effective demagnetizing devices and new minesweeping techniques alleviated the threat considerably. Nonetheless, the thought of falling prey to a blast powerful enough to sink a ship in a matter of a few minutes was unnerving to any seaman, whether experienced or a new recruit. Although naval mine usage was greatest in the areas around the British Isles, and especially in the English Channel, the RCN was well-prepared in applying its own defensive measures, especially near the major shipping ports of Halifax, St. John's, and Sydney.

## Deck Guns

AS CANADA'S INVOLVEMENT IN THE SECOND WORLD War progressed, the RCN fleet grew, in number as well as in size, from the tiny fairmile motor launches, to the much larger destroyers. Needless to say, the fleet was heavily laden with the varied armaments installed aboard ship. Aside from attack torpedoes and depth charges carried on most corvettes, frigates, and destroyers, there were also anti-aircraft guns, heavy assault guns, and machine guns of varying calibre.

Early in the war, River Class destroyers carried .5 calibre Mark III Vickers machine guns, single, twin, or quad mountings. They proved to be rather ineffective in warding off enemy planes and soon were replaced by the Mark II Browning version, which was much superior in distance, performance, and range. These Brownings were also used on RCN corvettes, frigates, minesweepers, fairmiles, and most other ships.

The 20-millimetre Oerlikon gun was also fitted to most RCN ships as a basic anti-aircraft armament which had an effective range of 3–4 kilometres. Also include in the arsenal of the Canadian destroyers and corvettes were 40-millimetre anti-aircraft "pom-pom" guns. The original Mark II version soon gave way to the much superior Mark VII model which

*Manning a two-pounder anti-aircraft gun while on convoy, July 10, 1940. At this early stage of the war, the few ships available in the RCN were ill-equipped.* (Library and Archives Canada PA-104057)

could fire up to 100 shells per-barrel, per-minute to a distance of 4.5 kilometres, clearly outperforming the earlier Mark II.

In the later years of the war, .56-calibre water-cooled Bofors guns were used extensively as they could fire up to 120 rounds per-barrel, per-minute to a distance of 10 kilometres,

*Bofor 40 Gun on the destroyer* HMCS Algonquin. *The Bofors 40 gun, a Swedish designed anti-aircraft weapon, used both on land and at sea, was one of the most popular and widely used armaments during all of the Second World War.* (Library and Archives Canada PA-204655)

a distinct advantage over those U-boats that chose to, or were forced to, remain on the surface and challenge any RCN ship bearing down on them. But the German subs had a variety of powerful deck guns at their own disposal, including the mighty 88-millimetre anti-aircraft gun, and all were trained in their use. In a shooting encounter, both sides relied on men who were well-trained, determined, and cool under fire.

The heaviest guns, used on the larger ships, were the three- and four-inch high-angle guns, the biggest aboard a warship and used for bombardment, covering fire, and any other major engagement requiring maximum firepower.

While the heavier guns were located fore and aft of the ship, the smaller machine guns were spread out where they were deemed most effective and would give a clear firing sweep.

Although the RCN had a slow and rather rough start, the now-experienced crews had, by war's end, proven themselves many times over as did the vessels they were on, especially the tough corvettes and their crews, who showed themselves to be as able as any seaman who sailed into the dark waters of the North Atlantic.

## ASDIC

FORTUNATELY AS HUMANS, WE ARE MOST OFTEN ABLE to learn from our errors, omissions, and ignorance; however, in many cases, this knowledge comes too late to avoid disaster. The *Titanic* tragedy of 1912 demonstrated the need for ships to have some kind of device to detect hazardous obstacles on or below the surface of the water. Within two years of the *Titanic* sinking, a primitive sort of echo sounder was being developed, and by 1916 hydrophones, which detected under-water sounds, were available, although direction finders were far from accurate. But research and trials continued at a furious pace until, in 1917, a prototype of the first underwater sound detection system, using quartz crystals, was successfully tested. The device was given the name ASDIC, said to be an acronym for Allied Submarine Detection Investigation Committee, although it was later shown that no such committee did actually exist.

ASDIC was basically a transmitter able to send out sound waves in a chosen direction. If the sound hit an object, it was reflected or echoed back to the transmitter. By calculating the speed, length of time, and direction of the object, such as a submarine, the distance and location could be detected.

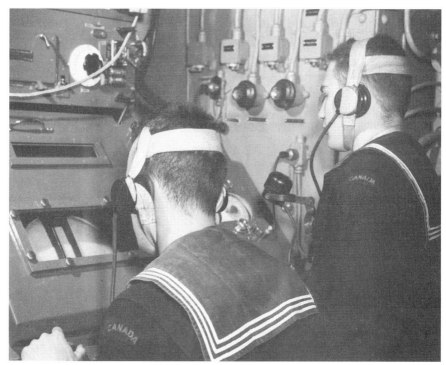

*ASDIC operators often had to work under challenging conditions which could make accurate readings difficult. With improved technology and training, reliability greatly improved.* (Library and Archives Canada PA-139273)

The ASDIC could also be used to listen to noises and to send out sound. Propeller movement could be picked up, as well as noises from compressed air in ballast tanks if a sub were changing depth. The transmitter was encased in a water-filled dome beneath the ship's hull—a precarious location, as quite often the hull would hit ice or a piece of driftwood and the ASDIC could be easily damaged or be knocked off completely. At the onset of the Second World War, just about every warship in the Allied fleets was equipped with these sonars, as later termed by the US navy.

The early ASDIC system had other drawbacks. Bad weather hampered a ship's movement and the tossing around in high seas resulted in poor readings; further, ocean currents, salinity content, sea ice, and even large schools of fish would throw off readings. And any speed over 18 knots resulted in poor contacts. The ASDIC system was also hampered by depth charges, which necessitated shutting down the ASDIC just before launching, in effect firing blindly with the targeted sub often escaping. But improvements continued with the advent of the multi-barrelled Hedgehog and later Squid, which were able to launch the depth charges without loss of ASDIC contact.

A reliable ASDIC operator was an absolute premium to a ship's crew, especially if he could sort out the differences between noise generated from ice, whales, schools of fish, and temperature and saline water variations from those of a ship or U-boat. A good operator could recognize the turning sounds of a ship's propeller as friend or foe. In the midst of a sub encounter and challenge, which could be quite prolonged and often took place in stormy conditions, the attacking ships were constantly on the move in all directions, firing depth charges and evading enemy torpedoes while trying to keep their convoy from being scattered. The very survival of these ships and their crews often depended on the overworked

ASDIC operators, for there was no real rest, as even in the roughest seas the threat of a U-boat was always present and a constant vigilance had to be maintained, especially at night. As the war progressed, the expertise of the operators and the newer, much improved versions of ASDIC were a significant factor in Allied successes in the Battle of the Atlantic. Never can enough be said in gratitude to these young volunteers, from farms, forest land, tiny fishing villages, and great cities across Canada, who contributed so much to the war effort.

## Radar

BY THE BEGINNING OF THE SECOND WORLD WAR, BOTH Britain and Germany had, in utmost secrecy, the development of basic radar systems well underway. In fact, the RAF had already been using their own system for coastal defence since 1940. The US coined the term radar from the acronym for Radio Detection and Ranging. Radar detection involves emitting radio waves from transmitters and reflecting them back via solid objects. The reflected waves are amplified through a cathode ray tube where they could be displayed visually, charted, and distance and direction calculated. At first, the shortest wavelength produced was 1.5 metres, much too broad to pick up small targets; however, technical improvements came quickly as the war progressed. By 1941 the RN was able to outfit most ships with a version which was able to reduce a wavelength to 10 centimetres, allowing a target as small as a sub's conning tower to be detected. Unfortunately, a Canadian version of Britain's breakthrough model only was available in 1943.

The RN and RCN monitored radio traffic from German U-boats and surface ships constantly, especially after the radio codes were broken. In fact, many naval historians believe it was the continued use of monitored radio communications between U-boats, vital for organizing wolfpacks, that led in great part to the downfall of the German submarine fleet. Between the Allied ships and airplanes, after 1943 most enemy subs were, through the use of radar and sonar, quite easily found, hunted down, and destroyed.

### Life in the Radar Shack

*I went to Halifax and joined the Canadian Navy. Most Newfoundlanders joined the RN. The RN only got 48 cents a day and the Canadian navy paid $1.25 a day, so it was a big incentive, you know, to go to join that navy. When we went to [HMCS]* Montcalm *in Quebec City, this was basic training. This would show you how to march and run and handle guns, and a few things like that. That took about six to eight weeks maybe; and then we were finished there, we were drafted to [HMCS]* Cornwallis *for advanced training, which brought you into gunnery and all the bigger stuff. When you'd finish that, you went up towards a selection officer to find out what branch you would like to go into.*

*I chose the radar branch; and then we were drafted to [HMCS]* St. Hyacinthe *in Quebec; and we did a three week radar course. From there on, I drafted aboard the [HMCS]* Galt *for one trip only and that, we completed our radar course. Then I drafted the [HMCS]* Fort Frances *two days later; and I never saw dry land afterwards. You know, we were quite new and we had the latest radar equipment that we knew of in those days which was 20271 [Type 271: air-surface warning system], which had 35, 40 miles capacity, so we could pick up an echo, depending on the size of the echo, of course. We were sure we had some secret parts of the*

*Signaller in cold weather. In the earlier stages of the war, radio, radar, and even* ASDIC *were not carried on many warships. Information had to be sent by light signals, in good weather or bad. With rapid advances in communications and detection technology, life was made a lot easier aboard ship.* (Library and Archives Canada E010775186)

*radar set; we didn't even know what it was, but nobody was allowed in the radar shack, only the operators, ourselves, and there were only six of us aboard ship. Our total crew was about 125.*

*Working on the radar, you worked four hours on and eight off was the shift. Then we worked a half hour on the set and a half hour off the set. When your half hour is off, you crawled underneath, because the radar shack was only about six by six, mostly, it wasn't that big, four by four; and there was enough room to lie down under the chair and have a nap. Because half hour on was the way we had to do it because of your eyes.*

*As senior ship in the convoy, we would zigzag, and back and forth. Most times, our convoys, we were taking were eight knots, and there could be anywhere from 50 to 80 ships in it. But our zigzagging, well, to use our words, taking a right and left cut on facing the convoy. We would zigzag back and forth and sometimes they'd use us for station keeping and you know, the nearest ship and all, any reports we had to give them.*

*—Ernest Hayward Winter, St. John's, Newfoundland, courtesy* The Historica Memory Project

## HF/DF (Huff-Duff)

THE ALLIED VICTORY IN THE BATTLE OF THE ATLANTIC was the result of combining several primary factors in the area of communication and detection. British radar and code-breaking advancements, in conjunction with high-frequency radio detection abilities, made life quite unbearable for most U-boat crews. By early 1945, U-boat kill and tonnage rates had decreased considerably while the number of subs put out of action was well over seven hundred.

HF/DF, or simply Huff-Duff, radio sets were being installed on many convoy escort ships by 1943. The principle of HF/DF was to intercept radio signals and determine their direction. Monitoring German naval traffic using HF/DF made it much easier to get a triangulated fix on U-boats in the area, even if a sub's location was over the horizon and beyond the field of radar. Once a location was deemed accurate, high-speed hunter-killer units comprised of ships and armed spotter planes would be on their way. If the sub submerged, then the ASDIC would be put in effect. German submarine commanders used radio extensively in organizing wolfpacks once a convoy was spotted and, for some reason, believed that if radio messages were short, detection would not be accurate. This assessment would eventually prove to be, arguably, the biggest mistake made by the German Kriegsmarine and disastrous for the otherwise capable officers.

Shore-based HF/DF stations were also constructed, making the locating of enemy ships much more accurate. By the end of 1943, the Battle of the Atlantic had turned in favour of the Allies, not only due to the Allied fire power, but to the successful detection methods which made it so much easier to locate, reach, and eliminate the powerful U-boats.

### Welcome aboard ship!

*I can remember the first time when I went from Halifax to Saint John, I wrote my mother and said, you can't imagine the size of these waves (because the only time I'd ever been on the water was out on Lake Erie, on a fishing tug). And I said, one moment you're up at the top, you can see for miles, the next moment, all you can see is water. We had all the stokers in our mess and, as I recall, I think there was something like either nine or ten. The two cooks were in our mess, two officer stewards, and what they call a sick bay tiffy [navy medic]. He was the medical type. And they all were billeted in that mess. So it got pretty cramped, especially when you hung your hammocks down there.*

*And the thing that I remember quite distinctly is that we'd sling our hammocks, fore and aft; and my feet would be facing aft, but the guy next to me, his feet would be facing forward. So we slept all the time with someone's feet in our face. And that got kind of nauseating at times, if you can imagine. It was quite interesting when we drew our food from the galley that come down on the trays, big deep trays and then we'd have to share with each other.*

*Stoker's mess aboard the HMCS* Kamsack. *With the call of action stations, this room dispersed quickly as young men fled to their assigned stations, ready for battle.* (Library and Archives Canada PA-204360)

*We each had a locker. It was only about three feet square and three feet tall. It was against the bulkhead. Each member there had his own locker, that's where we kept our personal gear. I was on patrol for quite a while up off Labrador, and did a bit of escort duty up to Iceland and back. Most of the time, it was just on the escort duty or patrol duty along the coast, and mid-ocean convoy. We had to go out one time and, one time I recall, when the transatlantic cable, there was something went wrong with that and we escorted a ship out there that brought the cable up from the bottom and they repaired it. And I was out I think something like seven or eight days on that.*

*The ship did get a mention. They'd won this battle honours by trying to get all the subs out of the Gulf of St. Lawrence before the big convoy went over. There was a convoy formed up at just south of Halifax. There's 125 ships involved. The length of the convoy was 10 miles and the width was two miles. And we did a patrol off of that convoy for a couple days before they actually took off. There was quite a bond developed between a person and his ship, you know. It was our home really.*

*—Don Birdsell, Hagersville, Ontario,*
*courtesy* The Historica Memory Project

## RCN Convoy Tactics

THE RCN'S OBJECTIVE IN ANY CONVOY OPERATION WAS obviously to have its ships arrive at their destination in a safe and timely manner. How to deal with the U-boats would, of course, depend on what tactical approach the enemy subs themselves would attempt. Much was still up in the air at the war's outset, as both the British and Canadian navies had expected to be dealing with larger marauding surface ships, not U-boats. Even with a zigzag sailing pattern and by deploying an escort ship at the stern, aft, and sides, six months later in early 1940, rising shipping losses would necessitate more serious convoy protection. But a submarine was very difficult to locate, let alone destroy. With so few ships available for convoy duty, as some convoys had a mere two or three ships to protect fifteen or twenty merchant carriers, an attack by a well-coordinated wolfpack could easily decimate a convoy. Using a merchant ship as "bait," hopefully to point to the location of a U-boat quickly, was rumoured to be a tempting but unspoken tactic, which the RCN was trying to avoid. Needless to say, any decision in this direction would not improve the already strained morale of the merchant marine service.

ASDIC was used but proved to have several drawbacks, especially in the waters of the Gulf of St. Lawrence. Attacks on

*View from the corvette* HMCS Chambly, *part of the first flotilla of corvettes heading to St. John's, on May 23, 1941. Note the carley float on deck ready for quick use.* (Library and Archives Canada PA-037447)

U-boats were most effective by aircraft, but there were too few in the early years of the war. The RCN was just not prepared for the 1942 onslaught, in which a mere handful of U-boats sank over twenty merchant carriers. Many of the new Canadian ships had been drained off the fleet to serve in the Mediterranean, in the Iceland sector, or along the main transatlantic shipping lanes. Britain could not risk having its main supply arteries severed. However, an impressive number of corvettes and frigates were being built, quickly deployed as convoy escorts, and would become instrumental in gaining superiority over the wolfpacks. Gradually, with more and more RCN ships becoming available, tactical hunter-killer units began showing their effectiveness on the Atlantic convoy routes.

Eventually, as the number of U-boats built increased, so did the number of these raiders put out of action. The advancements in ASDIC, radar, and radio detection, as well as the sheer number of well-armed ships and all-important long-range torpedo-carrying aircraft, resulted in workable and successful convoy tactics. The RCN was still losing ships by 1945, but the loss of enemy subs was rising rapidly as the war at sea raged to its final conclusion.

### Deadly Crossings

*Practically every crossing we had, we met some action from submarines. Most of the crossings, we lost one ship anyway. Later on during the war, it wasn't so hectic but to begin with, with the wolfpacks and in 1942, it was the peak of the U-boat warfare, we lost a lot of ships. On one crossing, we lost I think it was eighteen ships. But of the eighteen, there were thirteen submarines in this wolf pack. And so they were situated in together under and they waited for the convoy to pass over and then they would come up and start popping them off. And with six escorts, it was impossible to keep them out. So they took their toll. But the majority of our ships, we had convoys of eighty ships and so we lost eighteen.*

*Of course, that was bad because there would always be survivors and of course, we were always detailed, our ships were always detailed to pick up survivors if there were any. And we, first time we picked up in bitterly cold weather and stuffed with ice and we spotted one boat with one person in it and that turned out to be a fifteen-year-old Scottish lad. And we picked him up and he was pretty happy to be picked up but he was almost frozen. And he had a whistle in his mouth and he couldn't even blow it.*

*Other times, when we lost the 18 ships, we had about 80 survivors on our ship, which had been picked up, we'd haul them overboard. Some living, some dead but we'd bring them aboard and try and revive them. We'd all take our turn trying artificial respiration but normally we couldn't bring them back and of course, then you'd have some burials at sea. One sixty-six, yeah, that was a really bad one. Coast Guard cutter* Spencer *was one of our senior ships and he had found a submarine. And we were all involved in picking up survivors and carrying out attacks on the submarines. It wasn't easy to get an attack but it's pretty hard to bring them up and you have to be right on top of it. But you'd see any straggler merchant ships and you'd know for sure that they wouldn't be there the next day. But the German submarines, they just pulverized us and ship after ship was sunk. And naturally, we had to pick up survivors. And we carried them back on one submarine. We thought we had them but we were in the area just to pick up, or give some evidence that it was sunk and a lot of evidence came up, including some German sailors. And of course, we were just there in the vicinity and we got another ping, so that's a ping from another submarine. So naturally, we couldn't stay, so we just took off and didn't pick up any German survivors. That was something. It's not nice but it had to do because we were a sitting duck at that time.*

*It was so grim in the middle of the Atlantic in stormy weather, it's hard to describe how the ship can stay afloat. You'd be battering into waves and rolling, sometimes you'd roll almost to the point of rolling over and you'd keep on going and the up and down, it was just impossible. And of course, the mess decks aren't waterproof, they would come in somewhere, so we were a lot of times just walking in water. And of course, it's tiring too and you'd have to do your watch, you'd have to get up and go on action stations, whenever that happened, you'd still had to do your own watch, so it was pretty difficult. And the cook has a hell of a time, you know, it was, I don't know how he ever did it but he was such a great guy and he would do his best to make us comfortable and bake bread in the middle of the Atlantic. And I'm telling you, the smell of fresh bread in the middle of this is pretty, pretty nice.*

—*John "Tug" Wilson, Regina, Saskatchewan,*
*courtesy* The Historica Memory Project

# GERMAN WEAPONS AND DETECTION

## U-boats

HOW DID U-BOATS BECOME SUCH A SCOURGE TO NORTH Atlantic shipping? At the beginning of the Second World War, submarine warfare was anticipated to be but a minor threat to the powerful British navy, who assumed its radar system would make short work of a few pesky subs.

Germany had circumvented the Treaty of Versailles's ban on building a U-boat fleet by having subs built and crews trained in Spain and Russia. And in Germany itself, research into sub designs was not banned. By the end of the 1930s, Germany had at least fifty U-boats built. Admiral Karl Doenitz was successful convincing Hitler that with three hundred U-boats he could bring Britain to its knees. He was wrong. Germany got off to a quick start at the beginning of the war with major successes at Scapa Flow and the sinking of the battleships *Royal Oak*, *Courageous*, and a number of unescorted cargo ships. Further, the collapse of France in 1940 gave Germany access to several important naval bases. And with easy access to the Atlantic, U-boats could now reach far to the west, out of the range of Allied planes. Allied losses soon mounted, with over 1.6 million tons of shipping lost by November of 1940. These were the so-called "happy times" for U-boat crews. But the Germans could not put out new boats fast enough to keep up with Allied shipping. This gave Britain (and Canada) enough time to produce their own sub-fighting ships. From 1940 onward, both sides would concentrate on new and improved weaponry, radar, and sonar. In the long run, it would be the Allies who were able, especially with the effectiveness of radar-equipped long-range torpedo bombers, to take the upper hand against the U-boat fleet until. That is, until 1945, when U-boats were no longer considered a serious threat.

But the threat would remain until the end of the war, albeit on a much smaller scale. The German naval and submarine bases were coming under increasing attack by air and ground forces, as were the great steel mills and factories needed for submarine building. Much of the now shrunken U-boat fleet was being recalled to home waters to try and protect German bases. German recruitment was also becoming very difficult. Where once only well-trained, experienced, and qualified young men were accepted into what was considered an elite brotherhood, Doenitz's crews had dropped to desperate levels, losing, over the course of the war, nearly 30,000 of the 40,000 young men sent out on patrol.

A new sub type was produced as a last-ditch effort to defend against the Allied onslaught and was called the Type XXI, which had greater speed and better propulsion and endurance. But most importantly, these new models were coated with a rubber substance that supposedly absorbed ASDIC. Initially promised for use in November 1944, the first of these new subs was finally launched a week before the German surrender. Like the case of so many German "superweapons," it was a case of too little too late. Although the Kriegsmarine was beaten long before the war's end, the Battle of the Atlantic would prove to be the longest single engagement of the Second World War.

## Conditions Aboard

U-BOAT CREWS WERE AMONG THE MOST HIGHLY TRAINED of all German armed forces, made up of specialists in radio, weapons, and engineering. Generally, five years of training were required to crew a U-boat to Doenitz's satisfaction. With the Allied successes against German subs from the middle of the war onward, highly trained recruits were much harder to come by and combat casualty rates rose dramatically.

Comfortable living aboard a German sub was definitely not a priority. In fact, conditions aboard a U-boat were the worst of all German warships. Each patrol would spend up to six months at sea. During this period a crew member, cold and wet, could not shave, bathe, or even change clothes, as fresh water was limited. Privacy was non-existent with narrow bunks fitted next to, or on top of, the torpedoes, or crammed down the single aisle running the length of the ship. As torpedoes were expended, a bit more room was available for sleeping. Crews left their warm bunks to the men coming off their watch. Only the commander had a bit of privacy, with a small curtain covering his sleeping quarters which might be large enough to include a small writing table.

At the beginning of a patrol there was plenty of food, crammed into every nook and cranny, including the spare toilet. Fresh fruit and perishable food went first. But in the damp, humid air, food spoiled quickly, the bread quickly developing a whitish mould the men called "rabbit fur." After the fresh meat, hams, and vegetables were gone, there was left canned food which quickly absorbed the odour of diesel oil and was in fact called "diesel food" by the crew members. A single toilet was shared until the second one was clear of food. The toilet operated on a manual hand-pump system and could cause a lot of problems if not used carefully.

Although there was excitement during periods of enemy encounters, hunting a ship, or being hunted, much of a sub's patrol was filled with psychologically damaging boredom. Music was piped throughout the boat, men sang songs, played cards, chess, and other games to pass the time.

When and if the boat returned from its long patrol, the crews, dirty, most with long beards and filthy clothes, were welcomed ashore as conquering heroes, especially if the patrol was considered successful. Medals were presented and the young men were treated with the utmost respect and put up in the finest hotels, or delivered personally to their homes and families until it was time to leave on the next patrol.

## Enigma

MUCH HAS BEEN SAID AND WRITTEN ABOUT THE ENIGMA coding machine which was used extensively by German U-boat commanders in the Battle of the Atlantic. The machine, about the size and shape of a small typewriter, was developed secretly by the Germans at the outbreak of war. The Allies, of course, knew about the Enigma, as radio traffic between enemy subs was routinely intercepted. But until the code could be broken, the Germans, using Enigma, would still succeed in organizing the deadly U-boat wolfpacks, which continued to put Allied shipping in danger.

The British had obtained an Enigma unit from the Poles and set up the "Ultra Project," whose mission was to break the codes. Cryptography experts, headquartered at Bletchley Park, were brought in, including noted chess champions and mathematicians.

By 1941, there had yet to make significant progress. But, on May 8 of that year, a stroke of luck occurred as *U-110* was rammed by the RN destroyer HMS *Bulldog*. Thinking the sub was going down quickly, the crew abandoned ship. But the U-boat was sinking slowly, giving time for crew members of the *Bulldog* to board it with instructions to claim anything of value. Included in their "take" was a fully functional Enigma machine along with its instruction manual. The codes were soon broken and for a while the Allies knew of vital German shipping movements, concentrations, intentions, and strategy. But within a year, the Germans had updated Enigma, adding a fourth rotor, which in effect stopped the British decoders in their tracks. To make matters even worse, German decoders had broken the Allies' own Number 3 code used for co-ordinating escort ships and convoy traffic. German naval commander Karl Doenitz now had 126 operational U-boats, and successes picked up considerably.

It was not until early 1943, when the new Enigma code was finally deciphered, that the tide began to turn. Once again a retrieval effort to claim an Enigma machine from a damaged sub aided greatly in getting the decoding team at Bletchley on the right path. In this instance, the HMS *Petard* was among five British destroyers on the attack after U-559 was spotted off the coast of Port Said on October 30, 1942. The *Petard* pounded the German sub with depth charges until it lay on the surface, severely damaged, taking water, and foundering at a rapid rate. Despite this danger, three crew members, sixteen-year-old canteen assistant Tommy Brown, Lieutenant Anthony Fasson, and Able Seaman Colin Grazier, made several trips into the failing sub which was ready to take its final plunge at any second. The men were unable to retrieve the Enigma machine itself, which was bolted down tightly, but did manage to rescue several codes and books which were absolutely invaluable to the Bletchley team. Brown survived, but unfortunately Fasson and Grazier were seconds too late in escaping the sinking sub, and perished. Little did the three men realize how far-reaching would be the consequences of their acts of courage. With the aid of Enigma as well as Allied improvements in radar, radio detection, ASDIC, weaponry, and the sheer number of ships finally being made available, the British and Canadian navies were finally able to regain and hold the upper hand.

## Deadly Sabotage!

*After my training, I got drafted, the whole crew of a new ship about to be launched in BC, at Esquimalt; and we were shipped out seven days and eight nights by train. I've since been back by air. But the ship was delayed, so instead of being the second frigate (anti-submarine escort vessel) launched, we ended up being the third. We spent May, June, and July, and part of August, 1943 on the west coast. Dropped into Prince Rupert for a kind of a dedication ceremony. One guy composed a song about "they gave us cigarettes, a washing machine and guitar, but that's all they gave to the 'Fighting PR' [HMCS Prince Rupert].*

*From there, we came through the Panama Canal, up to Halifax, some more training off of Pictou, and then onto Newfoundland and Escort Group C3, mid-Atlantic, Newfie [Newfoundland]-to-Derry [run]. Four days in, turn around, and back. In March of 1944, we got assigned to go help the Yankee [United States Navy] escort group; and we took part in the sinking of a German sub [U-575; destroyed on March 13, 1944]. We picked up fourteen survivors: two officers, twelve men. I was a sentry looking after [them for] a few days. Most of them could speak English, and we got quite friendly. You know, they had the common enemy, the sea, the same as us. So we had lots in common to talk about. I found a very intriguing thing that I never forgot. Two of them were Lutherans. I'm a Presbyterian by birth, and they had praying mothers at home just like I had.*

*I got a rude awakening. We used to do supposedly thirty days out and four days in. But this time, we had gone forty-two and we were due in that night in Londonderry [Northern Ireland]. We were coming up the Irish Sea, picked up a sub on the ASDIC, and carried out two or three attacks, when all of a sudden, one of our Hedgehogs, turned out in the inquiry that it was sabotaged, it exploded when it left the mount, put the paint locker [flammable liquid storage room] and the forward mess on fire; killed six guys and wounded twelve.*

*We went into Belfast [Northern Ireland], but they wouldn't let us unload the dead and the wounded. They wouldn't allow us to have permanent berth on account of the dripping explosives. Some of the bombs had shrapnel all through them. I got involved with going into clean up the mess. I grew up in the country; and I butchered beef and pigs, and chickens, but I wasn't really prepared for something like that.*

*I was gathering up body parts in a dustpan and spewing in the other one. Could hardly stand up on that linoleum-covered deck for blood. I still wake up with nightmares; and smell that horrible stench of death and dismembered bodies. It leaves an awful imprint on you.*

—*George MacNair, Bathurst, New Brunswick,*
*courtesy* The Historica Memory Project

## German Weapons and Detection

THE GERMAN U-BOAT, IN RELATION TO ITS SIZE, WAS THE most costly naval ship in the German Kriegsmarine. The most common U-boat, the Type VII, used nearly every square inch available for engines, propulsion systems, radio, hydrophone, periscope and control center, galley and crew quarters, as well as torpedo armament and related guidance systems. On the sub's deck were anti-aircraft guns and deck guns of varying calibre.

The main weapon aboard a U-boat was the torpedo, a self-propelled tube carrying explosive payloads. Expensive to produce and highly sophisticated, these projectiles, 23.5 feet in length, carried a standard warhead of 617 pounds of TNT, enough to sink or seriously damage the largest of surface vessels. In the early years of the war, torpedoes often failed to detonate, or even to find their targets, and work on improving propulsion, guidance, and detonation systems was ongoing. Eventually, a reliable acoustic homing torpedo was developed; the Allies, however, who followed U-boat development closely, quickly came out with an anti-acoustic torpedo device called a Foxer, a noisemaker designed to throw a torpedo off course. As the Germans improved and developed their sensor accuracy, the Allies kept pace with their own improvements.

Germany's standard torpedo in the Second World War was the G7e series, all 7.16 metres in length and powered by 100-horsepower electric motors and lead-acid batteries, carrying a lethal 280-kilogram warhead. While the flaws in early models resulted in inconsistent and premature magnetic and contact detonation, design and performance were improved over the course of the war.

In 1943, the G7e T4 model introduced the first acoustic homing torpedo in which hydrophones mounted on the torpedo were automatically activated after straight running for 400 metres. The torpedo would then zero in on the sounds of a merchant ship's motor and attack. The T5 model was a much-improved version of the T4 and was called Gnat (German Naval Acoustic Torpedo) by the Allies. These models were able to zero in on the sounds of ships much faster than merchant vessels, putting larger cruisers and destroyers at greater risk. One serious drawback of the acoustic torpedo was the possibility of its being attracted to the sub or ship from which it was fired. This danger forced the U-boat to dive immediately after firing and go completely silent, making confirmation of a kill very difficult. Six-hundred-forty T5 Gnat torpedoes were fired in combat, resulting in the loss of 45 Allied ships. Eventually the threat was lessened to a great degree with the effective use of the Allies' Foxer.

### Torpedoed!

*June the 25TH, 1942, ship merchant vessel* Putney Hill, *was torpedoed at about 11:25 P. M., full moon. I didn't see the torpedo wake, even though I was on lookout on that side, but with the full moon it was probably not distinguishable because of the moonbeam's reflection, you couldn't detect any difference between the wake and the torpedo.*

*We were struck by a torpedo, blown up in the air, and I knew it was 11:25 because the lookout had just been in the wheelhouse and reported the time. And we both went up in the air, about three feet. The captain came out, said abandon ship and we went to the lifeboats. Both lifeboats on the port side had been blown up against the funnel and were useless. We went to starboard side, and now the ship had taken a big list of about forty degrees, forty-five degrees starboard. Two boats were in the water on that side. We went into the boats, twenty-two men. They immediately sank to the gunnels because it was a wooden boat and the strakes were open, not having been in the water for two years.*

*When the boat capsized, you looked at the small boat ahead of us and she was just in the process of doing the same. So here's two capsized lifeboats in the middle of the night. I can't swim but I do have a life jacket on and I saw the raft about fifty yards, a hundred yards away. And I know the swimming movements but I can't swim. But I did manage to get to the raft. I was the first on it. I helped to pull eight men on the raft.*

*Later on during the night, the U-boat [U-203] came alongside asking for the captain. We didn't know where he was. He went away and came back. He had on deck an apprentice of our ship. He spoke to the second mate, it had got a little bit rough now and this boy couldn't swim either, so I asked someone to come from the raft to the U-boat, to take him across. Which he did. His name was Hancock. When he got to our raft, it was very surreal. We said to him, Hancock, how the hell did you get onboard the U-boat? And it seems that he couldn't swim either but he found an oar which supported him. But a few minutes later, a naval gunner came and he also got on the oar which would not support that. So the consequences were they began to fight. And this kid won, I guess he kicked him in the guts or something and he disappeared.*

*So there he is, and the U-boat came alongside and he grabbed the ballast intake the U-boat has holes in the side for taking water. And they hauled him aboard and took him and interviewed him, and spoke English perfectly. The commander [Kapitänleutnant Rolf Mutzelberg], as it turned out, had been to the same bloody English school where this kid came from, Chelmsford in England. Unbelievable.*

*Anyway, he said to him, well, I'm going to put you back among your mates but don't come back again or the ending might be different. So he gave us some cigarettes, a pack of cigarettes and some matches. The kid couldn't swim, and the second mate went for him, so they gave these matches and cigarettes back to the crew because they would have been ruined.*

*Subsequently, when he was interviewed by the Admiralty in London, they gave him hell because he didn't know what brand the cigarettes were. They were trying to establish of course where the U-boat was being stored, supplies, was it Central America or something like that? So morning came, the two lifeboats which had been capsized had been righted, which you can do by giving the keel and rocking the boat until it flips.*

*I got in the captain's boat, there were no food in the raft, it had been stolen by the stevedores in Suez. But there was water, so we transferred the water and off we went. There were two men lost already, the assistant cook, he was seen hanging onto the propeller whilst he was still a little bit up like that. The other one was our gunner.*

*We saw the ship eventually go down, just like that. Might have got ahead of myself there. So after seven days in the lifeboat, the fourth engineer, who was on watch at the time of the torpedo, and had been burned by the hot oil dropping on him, over eighty percent of his body was burned, he died in seven days. So we proceeded for another two days and then we were suddenly seen approaching a British corvette called* HMS *Saxifrage. She was bearing down on us and the captain said he did not know we were there, we didn't know he was there, we were alone at the time, it was a pure fluke and he came alongside and he took us up on the nets, we climbed up the nets. We could hardly stand actually. Strangely enough, there was a kid onboard that corvette from my next village, he was a signalman and he gave me his bunk for the night and shaving and tackle and stuff like that.*

—*Alan Shard, Manchester,* UK,
*courtesy* The Historica Memory Project

German U-boats had a number of detection and communication systems available to help them set up attacks or to use in taking escape or avoidance measures. These included radar, hydrophones, sonar receivers, periscopes, anti-sonar coating, beacons, Enigma, and the schnorkel.

Radar was only established aboard U-boats in August 1942, after a Wellington that fell into German hands in the summer of 1941 was found to have an ASV Mk I Metox radar receiver. The Metox ended up giving the U-boats plenty of problems. Over the course of the war several improved models were put to use, but with limited success as improved Allied models became available.

Hydrophones were also extensively used on U-boats. These were relatively simple listening devices consisting of a pair of microphones which picked up the sound of a ship's propellers. By measuring the time and distance the sound took to reach the sub, the bearing of the vessel could be mathematically calculated, but not the speed or direction. A good radioman could also determine if the vessel was a warship or a merchant ship. But convoys could be picked up at a 100-kilometre distance, giving time to gather a wolfpack for a major attack.

U-boats, which could neither transmit nor receive messages while submerged, used a number of beacons to transmit messages to other subs. These included flare beacons, swimming beacons, and pre-recorded transmitter beacons which were released to the surface from a submerged U-boat. After the message was transmitted the beacon would sink itself.

With the improvements in radar, U-boats were finding it difficult to remain on the surface for any length of time before Allied radar spotted them. Diesel engines could not, of course, be used under water, and their batteries had to be charged on the surface on a regular basis.

Enter the schnorkel, which was a pipe with a one-way valve extending from the diesel engine when the ship was a few feet under water. Thus the intake and exhaust would serve the diesel quite well. Running just below the water's surface made it possible to elude enemy radar and avoid enemy aircraft. On the negative side, noise from the diesel made it difficult to use hydrophones and caused the periscope to vibrate violently. But overall, the schnorkel gave the beleaguered U-boat fleet another lease on life, albeit short. But developments in Allied radar soon made it possible to pick up even a schnorkel image.

## Combat Tactics

THE GERMAN KRIEGSMARINE USED A NUMBER OF ATTACK and evasion tactics in their attempt to cripple British shipping. In the early months of the war, before convoys came into effect, U-boats attacked single-cargo ships quite successfully and soon found the attacks at night were even more effective, at least until improved radar detection made night attack risky. If attacking a convoy, a single sub would, having slipped undetected into an ideal firing position, often fire multiple torpedoes in an array, hoping to hit two or even three ships at once. If fired from the surface, four spotters were assigned to pick up any movement from convoy and escort ships. These spotters were not permitted to even glance at the firing sequence lest they miss an enemy manoeuvre. Having fired its missiles, the sub would then speed off, or, if spotted, submerge quickly. Quite often ASDIC readings would not reliably pick up the U-boat as a threat, and the sub would get away clean and unscathed. U-boat commanders were also very skilled at detecting convoys, charting and plotting their direction and speed of travel, and calculating a correct interception point.

The use of the wolfpack attack method wreaked absolute havoc on Allied shipping. Use of wolfpacks only began after the fall of France, when Doenitz's fleet had gained access to the large French naval bases. Once a convoy was sighted, signals went out to all U-boats in the area to gather for the attack, each sub using its own preferred tactics. Some of these battles lasted three days or more, the U-boats often resting

*HMCS* Assiniboine, *on August 6, 1942, was rear escort of* Convoy SC-94 *when it spotted* U-210 *on the horizon. A running pursuit ensued, the* Assiniboine's *guns blazing furiously. Finally the* RCN *destroyer rammed and sank* U-210, *but not before the German U-boat's deck guns set the* Assiniboine *on fire, causing serious damage.* (Library and Archives Canada PA-037443)

by day and attacking at night. One or two of the escorts were usually attacked first, causing confusion and error. But the U-boats were relentless and the outcome could be devastating to the convoys.

One of the most damaging wolfpack attacks occurred on the evenings of October 16 to 19, 1940. In this case, Convoy SC7 was attacked by seven U-boats which managed to sink twenty of the thirty-four ships in the convoy. At the same time, Convoy HX79 was attacked with the loss of fourteen ships. In all, within a forty-eight-hour span, thirty-four ships were lost.

# RCN SHIPS LOST, 1940-1945

## 1940

A T THE ONSET OF HOSTILITIES IN 1939, THE GERMAN Kriegsmarine had free reign over Allied coastal shipping lanes, and targeted unprotected merchant ships at random. At this point, Doenitz had only thirty-nine U-boats available for duty, a far cry from the three-hundred he considered necessary, and yet tonnage losses were mounting rapidly. The strength of the fledgling RCN was waning, with most of the ships at its disposal assigned to protect the major Canadian shipping ports of Halifax, St. John's, and Sydney, as well as coastal waters. By mid-1940, the RCN, which was only able to supply two ships per convoy, had not yet lost a single ship, allowing Canadian shipyards time to complete the first order of much-needed corvettes. The loss of the RCN destroyer HMCS *Fraser* in June 1940 would be the first of twenty-four Canadian warships sunk by war's end.

## HMCS *Fraser*
*Destroyer, lost in collision, June 25, 1940*

IT MUST BE CONSIDERED A TRAGIC TWIST OF FATE THAT the HMCS *Fraser* affected the fates of the first three Canadian warships lost in the Battle of the Atlantic.

Built for the British Navy in 1931 and originally christened HMS *Crescent*, the 1,375-ton C class destroyer was sold to the RCN in 1936, and rechristened the HMCS *Fraser*. At the outbreak of war it was transferred to the Atlantic region to undertake convoy escort duties, serving admirably aside from an incident involving the HMCS *Bras D'Or*. This episode involved a collision on November 14, 1939, between the two ships at the entrance to Halifax Harbour. Damage was serious enough to put the *Fraser* under repairs for three weeks.

By May 1940, France was under siege by the German blitzkrieg and the *Fraser* was recalled to the French coast off Bordeaux to help evacuate area refugees. Accompanying it were the Canadian destroyer HMCS *Restigouche* and the British cruiser HMS *Calcutta*. The rough seas and poor visibility threatened to separate the three ships, and so the *Fraser*'s commander, Wallace Creery, ordered a course correction to bring them closer together. Somehow Commander Creery's signals and intentions were misread by the *Calcutta*, as the ships found themselves on a collision course. Noticing this much too late to avoid impact, the *Calcutta* sliced into the bow section of the *Fraser* like a knife into butter. The foredeck and bow of the *Fraser* broke completely away, bobbing like a cork in a tub of water. Injured men lay everywhere, yet many in other parts of the ship were not aware of the seriousness of the situation. Many thought a submarine might have rammed them. Sailors asleep in their bunks were knocked to the floor and, as the engine room flooded, power was lost and the lights went out.

The *Calcutta* dropped its lifeboats and stood by to pick up survivors, a difficult task in the darkness and oil-slicked water. Commander Lay of the *Restigouche* thought the *Fraser* may have taken a torpedo hit, or perhaps collided with a large rock, and returned to help retrieve men in the water or in lifeboats. Men still aboard the *Fraser* used scramble nets to climb to safety. The bow of the *Fraser*, severed and drifting away, finally flipped upside down in the water, spelling doom for several men trapped inside. As the few whaler boats continued to pick up survivors, many severely wounded, the small boats became overloaded. One of the rescuers fell into the deep and was lost, sinking quickly. The numbers of men still in the water began to thin rapidly as many sank quietly below the waves. Buoys, carley floats, and anything else that the men in the water could cling to, were thrown into the water. It was a fight against time, and the icy water was weakening the men fast.

The injured aboard deck of the *Restigouche* were many, suffering from burns, broken bones, and burning eyes, and choking on oil as the *Fraser*'s doctor, Blair McLean, and Stoker Tom Kellington worked hastily to alleviate pain by passing out tots of rum. The fatal collision resulted in the loss of forty-five of the *Fraser*'s crew, while nineteen crewmen of the *Calcutta* also died. The *Fraser* sinking has the very dubious honour of being the first loss of a Canadian warship in the Battle of the Atlantic.

### Man Overboard!

*We had an interesting experience off Iceland in March of 1945, with a convoy. There had been quite a storm. The ship was rolling heavily and we got a message from one of the other ships to say that there was a light, it was dusk, and there was a light astern to us. So the officer of the watch called the aft lookout to see if he could see the light. We were directed to go back and investigate. There was no answer from the aft lookout. So I went back. I guess I was still a second officer of the watch at that point.*

*Anyway, we went back and discovered that the aft lookout wasn't there. We went back and here was Able Seaman Robert Stewart, our aft lookout, in the water beside a light. What had happened, he had been in the heavily rolling sea, he had been flung over the side. He stood up for some reason or other, been flung over the side of the ship. As he went over, he grabbed the light off a carley float, a type of life raft, which was dangling at the side just below his aft lookout position. Because of the soot from the funnel, the line was deteriorated and it broke and came over with him. It was the type of light that had C cell batteries, and when it hit the water, it sloped upright, the light came on and he stayed by the light and that was the light that the ship in the convoy had seen.*

*Anyway, we came back to him. The captain brought us to about thirty feet from him and we looked down at him and at that point, he was sinking. He came to the surface again and then he was sinking. And the next thing I knew, I was in the water. I remember my training, a leading seaman giving his training, when we were doing the Officer Candidate Course, said, "Officers always look after their sailors." And I don't know what happened, but I remember him making the comment at the time and it struck home. Anyway, the next thing I knew, I was in the water beside him and got him, managed to pull him back up to the surface. He was in a duffle coat. I'd taken off my coat and was more manoeuvrable.*

*Anyway, then they threw a line for us and I grabbed the line and we hung on the side of the ship rolling as we did, banging against the bilge keel on the port side of the ship, which didn't hurt. He took quite a beating and I got hit too. They lowered a carley float, eventually got us back onboard the ship. He was put into sick bay, and eventually when we got to port, he was taken off to the hospital and spent a number of weeks in hospital getting better. I was better off than he was, although I gather I did pass out when I got back onboard the ship because I came to in the officer's bathtub with my captain, "Skinny" Hayes, pouring black rum down my throat. I was a teetotaler prior to that, but I soon became a drinker from that time on.*

—*Maurice Aikins "Migs" Turner, Winnipeg, Manitoba, courtesy* The Historica Memory Project

## HMCS *Bras D'Or*
*Lost in storm, October 19, 1940*

### Working Hard and Enjoying Life
*Unidentified crew member quoted from the* Windsor Daily Star, *October 31, 1940.*

*In 1939 Canada's navy was miniscule, with not nearly enough ships to effectively undertake the proper duties of protecting the Canadian coastline and considerable shipping traffic.*

*Until a substantial number of corvettes, frigates, and other warships became available, the* RCN *decided to requisition a number of vessels from other government and private sources. They were to be called Naval Auxiliaries and included fishing trawlers, private yachts, and other civilian and* RCMP *vessels, wherever they could be found. One of these ships was a former government-owned 265-ton trawler which was refitted as a minesweeper and rechristened the* HMCS Bras D'Or. *Short of regular* RCN *officers, a mixture of men from the fishermen's reserve and the merchant marine crewed the* Bras D'Or. *The Canadian navy desperately needed experienced officers, and while these men filled this requirement, the majority of the regular crew came from young men from all across Canada who volunteered to join the navy. The crew of the* Bras D'Or *soon found themselves busy with patrol and escort duties, as well as practising mine sweeping whenever they had time.*

*On June 10, 1940, Italy declared war against the Allies, and that same month the little converted trawler achieved a bit of a celebrity status as it captured the Italian freighter* Capo Noli *in the St. Lawrence River.*

*The* Bras D'Or's *complement of thirty was considered to be a happy and healthy lot and went about their duties without undue hardship or complaint. This was true among the whole crew, from the genial and capable commander, Lieutenant C. A. Hornsby,* RCNR, *on down. The crew had a twelve-piece orchestra, led by Able Seaman E. J. Pelletier,* RCNR. *Their cook, G. T. Ellis,* RCNVR, *was a professional boxer who excelled in inter-ship matches. One young crew member wrote home saying they were a "happy ship" and every one was "working hard and enjoying life." There were detractors, however, who insisted the trawler was a far cry from the warships that were badly needed. On November 14, 1939, at the mouth of Halifax harbour the* Bras D'Or *collided with the destroyer* HMCS Fraser. *Blame was initially put on the* Bras D'Or, *citing lack of crew experience, but an in-depth inquiry quickly overturned the findings, concluding that the* HMCS Fraser *commander, W. B. Creery, had been at fault through negligence.*

*On October 19, 1940,* Bras D'Or *was on regular patrol duty in the Gulf of St. Lawrence, escorting the Romanian cargo vessel* Ingener N. Vlassopol *from Baie Comeau to Sydney, Nova Scotia. Though travelling together, a vicious storm came up and the two ships were separated in heavy seas, although the* Bras D'Or's *lights could still be seen. But at 0350 hours, the second officer of the Romanian ship noticed the light from the* Bras D'Or *suddenly blink out. The officer was not concerned as he assumed the little minesweeper had simply darkened ship.*

*Neither the* Bras D'Or *nor any of its crew were ever seen again. The most widely accepted theory is that* Bras D'Or *was hit with a rogue wave, floundered and went down. The lack of flotsam or bodies suggested it sank immediately without time to launch lifeboats. While detractors claimed the ship was not seaworthy, its experience in heavy seas proved otherwise. It was rumoured to be experiencing some sort of engine trouble just before its last sailing. Further, the* Bras D'Or *had grounded on a 'mud and rock bottom' off the Rimouski wharf on October 18, 1940, but was successfully refloated at high tide. Perhaps some unreported damage to the hull occurred, weakening it considerably. The ship's Engineering Officer, Lieutenant M Cumming,* RCNR, *had also inspected problems in the engine room and signalled only that he was making "repairs and adjustments." The fact was, nothing could be effectively shown as the direct cause of the* Bras D'Or's *disappearance. What is known, however, is that the little ship and its happy crew were the first* RCN *ship lost in Canadian waters during the Battle of the Atlantic.*

*The loss of the* Bras D'Or *has never been forgotten, and in honour of the* Bras D'Or *and its crew the Canadian Navy, in 1961, christened a new revolutionary hydrofoil the* Bras D'Or.

The list of the men lost with the HMCS Bras D'Or is as follows:

Walter G. Armes

George W. Brenton

Walter J. Brown

Joseph P. L. Barton

Harold G. Chaddock

Harold G. Clancy

Elward R. Conrad

Malcolm Cumming

Joseph F. D'Entremont

William J. Doherty

Gerald K. Ellis

Gilbert W. Gordon

John W. Hacker

Leonard Hill

Walter M. Hillier

Charles A. Hornsby

Hugh J. F. Jones

William D. Keating

Ib Korning

Clarence L. May

Harry Murphy

Joseph E. R. Pelletier

Guy D. Petipas

Herman Ruel

John J. Stasin

Joseph E. Stewart

Gordon W. Walters

Matthew Watson

Miles L. Webb

James L. Young

### Desperate Rescue

*One of the things I experienced when I first arrived in Halifax—I was sent down there to get a ship and so I was waiting in the barracks for a while, but the very first day that I arrived there was a—outside what they called the gates of Halifax. They had a gate that they would let up to let the ships in, they would form when they were forming the convoys. Just outside there, one of the Canadian ships was sunk by a submarine and so everybody, all the ships in the harbour, all the navy ships, were sent out to see if they could catch this submarine. I was not on one of the ships but the guys afterwards were telling me about it. And they're guys who had—a corvette, only had about one hundred twenty sailors on it as I recall and they were pretty small ships. And these guys were in the water. They had life vests on but the north Atlantic is very cold and the ships that were sent out weren't allowed to go slower than about I think it was twelve knots, because if they can keep up a speed of let's say fifteen knots, then the torpedoes wouldn't hit them. For some reason or other they just couldn't aim the torpedoes well enough. So a lot of the ships couldn't go really slow enough to really pick these guys up and they were throwing ropes over them and the guys too cold from being in the water even a short time, that they couldn't hold onto the ropes and they could hear them calling to be saved but not one of them was saved."*

—*Frank O'Hara, Silver Centre, Ontario,*
*courtesy* The Historica Memory Project

### HMCS *Margaree*
*Destroyer, lost in collision, October 22, 1940*

*"There was no noise at all, not even the sound of escaping steam."*
—*Lt. Bill Landymore. Excerpt, "First Blood in the*
*Navy," part 24, Marc Milner, November 2007*

BY LATE SUMMER OF 1940, BRITAIN WAS UNDER GREAT pressure as Germany turned its attention from attempting to destroy the Royal Air Force to that of bombing British cities, in an attempt to break the morale of the island nation. Invasion was still in the German plans, but they knew that breaking the will of the British people would go a long way, especially if the country could be completely blockaded as well. Therefore, in an attempt to force Britain to its knees, an all-out assault was ordered against its merchant shipping. Several convoys had been attacked in August, September, and well into November. Losses mounted quickly as merchant ships were sunk at an incredible rate. In one raid on October 17, a German wolfpack of six U-boats sunk fifteen of convoy SC-7's thirty-four ships. That same night, U-boats got twelve ships from convoy HX-79 in their sights, sinking all of them. The escorts assigned to these convoys were frustrated and exhausted by their efforts. Communications between ships, especially freighters, were usually poor, as often even radio communication equipment needed upgrading and, in some cases, was missing entirely. The seas were usually treacherous; often fog banks prevailed and collision was always a threat.

The surviving members of the HMCS *Fraser*'s crew were reassigned to the HMCS *Margaree*, which, after refitting, sailed out of Londonderry on October 20 to take up duties with the small convoy OL-8, consisting of only five ships and heading for Canada. By the evening of October 21, all five ships were well underway, the *Margaree* being the lone escort. The night was clear and the ships cut through the Atlantic at a fast clip of fourteen knots. At this speed it was decided that zigzagging would not be necessary.

The small convoy was sailing in two columns, one each of two and three ships. The SS *Port Fairy* and SS *Jamaica Planter* were both off the *Margaree*'s port bow. By midnight the weather had worsened considerably, the visibility such that the five ships could not be seen, visual contact broken as they split up. Then, at 0100 hours, tragedy struck: seemingly out of nowhere the *Port Fairy* appeared, crossing the *Margaree*'s bow. There was no time to take evasive action as the *Port Fairy* sliced into the *Margaree*, taking off its foredeck and bridge. Unlike the *Fraser* collision, in which the bow remained afloat for some time, the forward section of the *Margaree* sank immediately, taking anyone below deck or on that section down with it. The accident happened so quickly that most survivors didn't even hear much noise, save for the rending sound of tearing metal against metal.

Sub-Lieutenant Bob Trimbell and Able Seaman H. V. Holman were quick in their reactions, going aft at once to disarm the depth charge settings. Within seconds 142 men and officers were lost. Thirty-four survived the initial collision, but two of these men were crushed between the two ships as they tried to scramble up to safety on the *Port Fairy*. It was hard to determine exactly what caused the massive collision, as all those on the bridge were lost. Although weather was undoubtedly the prime factor, it was considered that a faulty compass or simply an error in navigation may have contributed to the collision. Unfortunately, the cause will never be known. What is considered truly heartbreaking is the fact that eighty-six of the *Margaree* dead were survivors of the HMCS *Fraser* collision of June 25.

# 1941

WITH THE FALL OF FRANCE IN 1940, THE U-BOAT THREAT, now using captured bases, increased considerably. Doenitz's fleet were now able to move far beyond Allied air protection, where, using wolfpack tactics, they wreaked havoc on merchant convoys in the "black hole" of the mid-ocean. The RCN's fleet, with the arrival of the much-needed sub-fighting corvettes, was growing steadily, but the young crews were being worked to exhaustion, losing four warships in 1941.

## Fighting in the "Black Hole"

*My name is Jack Smallwood. I was born in the year, 21st November, 1919. Well, as you know, Bedford Basin is just off Halifax. It's a huge basin, you'll see it coming into Halifax. And at one time, there was 156 ships in there. It was loaded. And that's the time I was on the HMCS Skeena, that would be in November of 1940. We started out, we came into Halifax harbour and then we started from there. And we were the escort and we went to about the worst place there could be in the North Atlantic, called the black hole. It was the worst place that could ever be. I saw 17 ships go up in 36 hours. We never hit our hammock or ever had a sleep on. And it was quite thrilling.*

*But anyway, we escaped and came back...to Halifax, before we went to the Avalon Peninsula. And every time we went back from Avalon, we would pretty well go through that danger zone. The German submarines were there, they were very brilliant. They would be about fifty feet below us, one-hundred feet and huge. If you didn't know, if you put your depth charge off at fifty feet, you could blow the stern off your own ship. And they would probably...stay underneath it until we pretty near got into Halifax.*

*We would try to interrupt some of the signals from the other German ships and submarines mostly but then it went on like that for some time. It was very successful. In the morning, there'd be rum issued, which was the old black rum that I could buy for $18 a gallon. And I'd pump that up into wicker jars and service the ship's company. The mess deck would get two parts water and one part rum. Some captains said three parts water and one part rum. The Chief P. O.'s [Petty Officers] got it neat, got it straight. And they'd take it back to their mess and probably...they drank it. At 11:00,* *the piper would pipe "Up Spirits." All hands onboard for "Up Spirits." And some of the boys coming off watch and that, it certainly went down right, it warmed their stomach.*

—Jack Dewar Smallwood, Charlottetown, Prince Edward
Island, *courtesy* The Historica Memory Project

### HMCS *Otter*
*Armed yacht, destroyed by fire, March 26, 1941*

THE TRAGIC LOSS OF THE HMCS *OTTER* AND NINETEEN of its crew on March 26, 1942, illustrates clearly that direct confrontation with the enemy is not necessary to suffer losses in wartime. Experienced sailors have long realized that the forces of nature, unforgiving and indiscriminate, are not to be trifled with, especially on the raging seas off Atlantic Canada.

By March 1941, Allied shipping was taking heavy losses. The lack of RN and RCN warships was so substantial that only two or three could be made available as escorts for each convoy setting out across the Atlantic. These convoys were under constant threat of attack from Doenitz's wolfpacks, especially in the sectors near Britain and France. With so few ships available, the RCN was forced to press civilian vessels into service since corvettes and frigates, now coming out of the shipyards, were quickly being sent to the areas of more concentrated U-boat traffic. Still, it was vital that the major ports of Halifax, St. John's, and Sydney be protected. One of the ships designated as a harbour and coastal patrol boat was a former luxury yacht, already twenty years old, at 419-tons and 160 feet in length. Rechristened the HMCS *Otter*, the aging yacht, although steel-hulled, had a super structure built entirely of wood. The crew of five officers and thirty-six men was mainly from the Halifax area and for the past several months had been content with patrolling the entrance to Halifax Harbour, continuously on the lookout for subs or deadly mines. They had been successful so far, but U-boats were causing all kinds of havoc to the east, and you never knew when they might appear in closer waters. By March 26, the men of the *Otter* were pleased that they were doing their part in the war effort, and doing it well. Shore leave was frequent, conditions were comfortable aboard ship, and all was well. That was soon about to change.

On that date, the *Otter* found itself near Sambro Island, awaiting a rendezvous with a British submarine. At about 0830 hours on March 26, an explosion occurred in the engine room of the *Otter,* followed by a flash fire, later determined to have started in the generator. The fire spread through the wooden deck quickly as crew members desperately attempted to beat back the now raging inferno. But it was too late and the men were forced to evacuate, using two lifeboats and one inflatable raft. Captain Dennis Mossman, after seeing his men off the ship safely, joined one lifeboat of fifteen men. A Polish freighter that had appeared on the scene was able to get up close to this lifeboat, drop its rope ladders, and successfully get all sixteen men aboard. There were still two groups in the water, one lifeboat and a small inflatable raft called a carley float.

Within a short time a British sub arrived and, spotting the bobbing carley float, nestled up as close as it could to pick up survivors, heaving over a lifeline. Sadly, out of the fifteen aboard the raft, eleven had already succumbed to the elements. Of the four remaining survivors, three were in terrible shape and could not last much longer. Able Seaman Thomas Guildford, though weakened himself, was able to fasten a rope around each of his mates so they in turn could be hauled to safety. When it came Guildford's turn, the raft had drifted away from the sub, now out of reach of the lifeboats' ropes. Guildford was exhausted, cold, and weak, and could do no more. Aboard the submarine, First Lieutenant Merrick was not about to give up on his fellow seaman. Grabbing the lifeline, he quickly dove into the water, swimming thirty yards to the drifting raft, quickly fastened the rope around Guilford, and swam like mad back to the sub before he too became too weak to continue. Both Merrick and Guildford made it.

That left one other lifeboat unaccounted for. Seaman Jimmy Noade was the last man to scramble into lifeboat number one, making a total of eleven. Now it was a matter of waiting for help to arrive and trying to stay dry. The same Polish cargo ship which had rescued the other lifeboat now arrived, rope ladders were quickly dropped over the side. Safety was merely seconds away, but a large wave caught the boats just as a sailor was reaching for the rope ladder. The lifeboat flipped completely over, throwing everyone into the frigid water. The freighter quickly tried to lower its own two lifeboats, but the seas, now being churned by gale-force winds, resisted, and the two lifeboats were smashed to pieces against the freighter's hull, severely injuring one of the Polish rescuers. Noade and his fellow crew members fought frantically to upright their boat. They finally succeeded in getting the small boat turned back over and climbed in, but only four, including Noade, remained alive.

Now the weak, soaking wet, and miserable men could only pray that the freighter had not lost sight of them. Suddenly, it appeared once again, close by, its ladders waiting, but time was running out for Jimmy Noade and his group. Chief Officer Walker was only a few minutes from rescue, but was unable to hang on. Everett Gillis, the *Otter*'s chief motor mechanic, had succumbed earlier. There now remained only Noade and Tommy Ward, and for both it looked like the end was nigh. Though the rope ladders were within grasp, neither man had the strength to reach out and grab hold. Then, like the submarine hero Merrick, a Polish sailor stepped forward, tying a rope around his waist, signalling to be lowered down to the lifeboat. Tommy Ward, in bad shape, but alive, was quickly fastened and sent up. Jimmy Noade soon found himself aboard his rescuers ship and on his way to recovery.

The final death toll from the HMCS *Otter* tragedy was nineteen men, but it was recognized that if not for heroic efforts of several men that fateful day, many of the twenty-two other sailors would not have survived.

## HMCS *Levis*
*Corvette, torpedoed September 19, 1941*

BY LATE 1941, THE ALLIES WERE STILL IN DESPERATE need of more ships, and shipyards were being pushed to turn out more corvettes, patrol boats, and frigates. As a result of this pressure, some ships were commissioned and declared ready for service despite many being under-armed and not fully fitted, lacking canvas weather protection, or even proper ASDIC equipment. Such was the case of HMCS *Levis*.

The *Levis*, a Flower Class corvette commissioned in May 1941, was taking part in convoy escort duties by September 19, 1941, despite having no anti-aircraft guns in its aft decks, no working gear for magnetic mine protection, and a damaged ASDIC dome, preventing it from normal screening. On this date, and despite these shortcomings, the *Levis* was four days out and about 190 kilometres east of Cape Farewell, Greenland, in only its second eastward crossing, acting as an escort in convoy SC-44. The *Levis* carried a complement of 58 officers and crewmen.

At 0205 hours, U-74, under the command of Eital-Friedrich Kentrat, who was on his fourth Atlantic patrol, fired a torpedo at the HMCS *Levis*. Seaman Norman Fraser, on lookout that night, spotted the incoming torpedo, as did the lookout from the *Levis*'s sister ship the HMCS *Mayflower*. But it was much too late for evasive action as the torpedo slammed into the *Levis* about ten feet from its bow. All but two ratings on the stokers' mess deck were killed outright, and the first two bulkheads were flooded. At least ten men remained on deck and were later picked up by another boat. Lieutenant C. W. Gilding, commander of the ship, immediately ordered the heavily damaged corvette abandoned, a move that was to result in severe reprimands for Lieutenant Gilding. The *Levis* had not sunk immediately, and Gilding had left before all his men, not attempting to return to the ship to assess fire and bulkhead damage and possible repair, all standard at-sea procedures. In the absence of Lieutenant Gilding, Lieutenant Ray Hatrick took charge immediately, assisting the injured, ordering the depth charges to be reset to safe, and reassuring his men lest panic ensue. For his steadfast command and cool leadership under great stress, Hatrick was recommended for the Distinguished Service Cross.

The HMCS *Mayflower* towed the *Levis* for five hours before it was cut loose to disappear below the waves. All ninety-one survivors were taken to Iceland to recuperate for ten days. In all, eighteen men lost their lives on the ship. The HMCS *Levis* would be recorded as the first Canadian corvette and warship to be lost to enemy action. The fate of U-74 was no better, as it was lost with all forty-seven crew members on May 2, 1942, after being hit with depth charges from a pair of British destroyers.

## HMCS *Windflower*
*Corvette, lost in collision, December 7, 1941*

ESCORTING CONVOYS ON THE NORTH ATLANTIC RUN WAS never easy, especially during the winter months when the raging seas always seemed to be at their most treacherous. Maintaining a tight, well-spread diffusion of both escort and merchant ships required constant vigilance, as the weary crews were well aware of the unremitting threat of German wolfpacks. But on the night of December 7, 1941, it was neither U-boats nor violent weather which spelled the end of the escort corvette HMCS *Windflower*.

On December 4, 1941, convoy SC-58 had departed Sydney, NS, eastbound for Liverpool. On reaching the Grand Banks, the convoy was taken over by the Newfoundland Escort Force (NEF), led by the destroyer HMCS *St. Laurent*. Six corvettes, including HMCS *Windflower*, were escorting the large convoy of fifty ships. By December 7, convoy SC-58 was sailing along quite smoothly, but engulfed in a heavy fog bank, not uncommon to the area, especially at that time of the year. Visibility was extremely poor as ships kept disappearing into the fog and reappearing unexpectedly. Aboard the *Windflower*, radar was being used to monitor its position in relation to the fleet, or at least its closest ship, since radar in 1941, especially in these circumstances, was still quite imprecise.

The *Windflower* had lost visual contact with the nearest ship on her port side, and its crew had assumed it had drifted off to starboard and would have to turn to port to regain proper position and visual contact. The *Windflower* cut sharply to port instead of merging smoothly into the column. This mistake proved fatal as out of the dense fog emerged the Dutch merchant steamer *Zypenberg*, a mere four-hundred yards off the *Windflower*'s port side. Although both ships immediately tried to manoeuvre desperately, it was too late. The *Zypenberg* sliced into the *Windflower* at a 45-degree angle, quickly shearing twenty-five feet off its stern. The hapless corvette did not sink immediately, giving time for crew members to reset depth charges, reduce steam pressure, and lower lifeboats safely.

Just as it was thought the damaged aft bulkhead might hold, allowing the ship to be brought under-tow safely, the bulkhead collapsed. The boiler had not had nearly enough time to cool and exploded violently as cold water reached the hot metal, resulting in most of the fatalities. Several men attempting to lower the lifeboats were caught in the blast and blown overboard. At 0950 hours the *Windflower* took its final plunge, leaving in the frigid, albeit calm, waters a morass of wreckage amongst which several dozen men thrashed and struggled frantically to survive. The *Zypenberg* went into action at once, quickly getting its boats down to reach the men. The water's temperature was around one degree Celsius, and the desperately flailing crewmen would clearly not last longer than mere minutes. In all, forty-seven men were rescued, but twenty-three died, either from injuries or succumbing to the numbing cold.

Another ship, the HMCS *Nasturtium,* had heard the boiler from the *Windflower* explode and rushed to the scene and launched depth charges, mistaking ASDIC contact with the sinking *Windflower* for a U-boat. In attacking the assumed sub, the *Nasturtium* received serious damage when one of its depth charges set off the *Windflower's*. As convoy SC-58 carried on its way, both the *Zypenberg*, with the *Windflower* survivors, and the damaged *Nasturtium* headed back to St. John's.

Although several ships of the RCN were lost or severely damaged in at-sea accidents, the *Windflower* was the only corvette lost in this fashion. Considering the number of RCN corvettes eventually involved in the war at sea and their huge contribution, a single major accident, though tragic, must still be deemed extraordinary.

### Warm Beds, Cold Steel!

*The convoys, the basic convoys that we were talking about were the ones that formed up in Halifax.... [T]he merchant ships would assemble in the Bedford Basin in Halifax, a large bay at the west end of Halifax or the Northwest end of the Halifax harbour. Our commanding officers of our ships that would be tied up at the jetties in Halifax, would get their orders to assemble and meet the skippers of the large merchant ships. And they would decide on the route that the convoy would take and the speed and the four ships, Canadian vessels that would protect the convoy.*

*A vessel like the* St. Croix *[...] would be at the front of the convoy and three other smaller ships including mostly corvettes would be on either flank and one at the rear. And they would go back and forth and up and down the convoys listening for and acting on attacking any submarines that they happened to infringe in within the territory of the convoy.*

*We've taken convoys over as many as 105 ships which would stretch 15 miles across the surface of the ocean and about the same width and with ample space in between, of course. But the speed of the convoy would maybe be 5 knots or 6 knots because of the size of these vessels and the weight of the armaments they were carrying. And our job was constantly to be on alert because the submarines were there. We knew they were there and if we ever picked them up, then it would be a matter of taking action and which it did.*

*I'll give you a quote about one winter night that, November of 1943, when we got our call to underwater action, because there's a difference between underwater action and surface action and aerial attack. We never got aerial attack. Not in our convoys. But all of our attacks were under water. Submarine attacks.*

*And on a ship, everybody including the cooks, had an action station. Like, no cook is going to be in the galley cooking food when the ship is fighting a submarine. So even the cooks have an action station [...] when I got my action station, I was a radio operator. But on an action station the leading signalman, the telegraphist, was the one that went to the radio shack and the other telegraphist had action stations. My action station was on the stern, dropping depth charges off the back or stern of the corvette.*

*So I got out of my hammock. I was in my skivvies, my shorts and my undershirt and I ran up on the deck in my boots and it was freezing cold but I went down the deck to my action station and when I was at the action station getting ready to drop depth charges, one of the officers threw a sheep skin coat around my shoulders and around my back to keep me warm. He saw me in my undershirt and shorts and I was freezing but he took his own coat off and threw it around my shoulders and I appreciated that. I can never recall which officer it was because I didn't even turn. We were involved in action and I didn't even turn to thank him to see which one it was and I never found out. But it was a memory that I had.*

*And just at that time in the middle of the night, one of the vessels went up in a ball of flame and we picked up the echo of the submarine and chased the submarine. We dropped depth charges. We never found out whether we were successful or not. The submarines sank two vessels in the convoy and surprisingly right in the middle of the convoy, they'd snuck through [...] but the convoy continued [and] we never picked up another echo when we were with them.*

*But it can happen anytime and anywhere and in that same convoy, we got our instruction from the captain of the leader of the escort that one of our lookouts picked up a single ship miles across the water off our starboard side. And we were given permission to break escort and to go over to find what that vessel was. And we challenged it by flashing a letter of the alphabet with our light [...] they would normally answer it, but nobody did. The vessel was dark and we approached from the stern and it was a massive merchant vessel. And when we rounded the stern to come up the side of it, the entire bow or the front of the ship was missing. The edge, the front of the bridge and back, the back half of the ship was still floating on the ocean but the front half of the vessel was gone. And we came to conclusion that the force of the wind and the waves, the vessel broke in two and the bow sank and the rest of the vessel floated. The crew had abandoned the vessel and all the boats were gone, the sea boats. But we came upon one a few miles ahead with about eight men in a boat and we went up alongside and took the survivors into the vessel and they stayed with us until we returned to Halifax.*

—*Robert C. Nelson, Hamilton, Ontario, courtesy* The Historica Memory Project

# 1942

THE YEAR 1942 WAS TERRIBLE FOR THE RCN AS THE German U-boat raiders found new and ripe targets just off Canadian shores in the Gulf of St. Lawrence.

By the end of 1941, convoys setting out from Halifax, Sydney, and St. John's were managing to hold their own against an equally determined U-boat fleet, primarily because the number of available Allied escort vessels was increasing, and these were put into service immediately. But, with the entry of the United States into the war in December 1941, the Eastern Seaboard, with its increased shipping tonnage, became a new and prime target for German U-boats, especially since the US was drawing away many of its warships and escort vessels to what were deemed high priority areas, primarily the Pacific. With Admiral Doenitz's subs now pressuring these American seacoast routes as well as those convoy lanes leaving Eastern Canadian ports, the lack of proper escort ships was making life very difficult for the RCN. Furthermore, the terrible Atlantic winter battered both the escort and merchant ships relentlessly. The majority of the convoy routes involved sailing through the icy darkness of Arctic seas south of Greenland. The crews knew they would be at the complete mercy of cold and ice, even if they had to go to lifeboats unharmed, as the freezing conditions could mean death in as little as five minutes.

The convoys, especially the vital oil tankers, as well as munitions, weapons, and troopships, had to be protected. Allied convoys were reaching as far as the great ports of Murmansk and Archangel in Russia, from the Bering Sea to the Gulf of Mexico, and from Gibraltar to South Africa. The war at sea was truly global, and neither side was about to give in. The shipyards in Canada and in Britain were running at full capacity, putting out badly needed corvettes, frigates, minesweepers, and destroyers. Yet it was still not enough. Calling the period from January to July 1942, the "happy time," German subs decimated the east coast shipping lanes, sinking four hundred merchant ships with the loss of only seven U-boats, and, until the Americans made more escorts available, the RCN would have to assist in protecting these routes as well.

The Germans, undoubtedly, were aware that the major convoy departure points were Montreal and Quebec City up along the St. Lawrence River. Convoys departed these cities continuously, heading for the marshalling yards in Nova Scotia and Newfoundland. The German Admiralty seemed not to consider the Canadian territorial waters of the Gulf of St. Lawrence area relevant compared to the open waters of the best-known Atlantic convoy routes. No plans had been prepared for dealing with Gulf traffic. Perhaps the Germans realized that Allied cargo could, if necessary, simply be routed by train to major ports in Nova Scotia and New Brunswick. Earlier attacks in this coastal zone seemed to happen only when opportunities presented themselves. Meanwhile, the RCN prayed this busy area would continue to be ignored. As it stood, many convoys on the Quebec and Montreal run were provided with only one escort, if any at all. The war still felt far away to most Canadians, who had not stopped to consider that the Germans might actually be a threat to their homeland. The RCN's fears would soon prove legitimate, as, over the next six months, Doenitz's Kriegsmarine set its lethal sights on the virtually unprotected ships plying the Gulf of St. Lawrence.

Needless to say, the people living along the shores of Gaspé and the St. Lawrence were shocked, outraged, and frightened to see the war unfold before their very eyes as explosions erupted for days just offshore, scattering wreckage and bodies along the coastline. These direct attacks were the first against Canadians within their own territory since the War of 1812, causing much consternation in Ottawa and Quebec, as many critics felt Canada's shipping was being sacrificed to provide protection to Great Britain.

Despite the five corvettes added to the Gulf naval force, it was still plain to see that protection was pathetically inadequate. On the Gaspé shore, the number of lookout towers was increased, and they were manned on a twenty-four-hour basis. Further, several thousand volunteers came forward to establish foot patrols. The threat of an enemy landing was not taken lightly by anyone, including the Canadian government.

The month of September 1942 was horrendous for both merchant ships and escorts alike as *U-517* and *U-165* put on a two-man show over a two-week period, sinking eleven vessels, including two RCN warships. The daring of these U-boat commanders was not to be denied as by the end of October, two more cargo ships went down to enemy torpedoes, including the SS *Caribou*, which was carrying civilians. The Gulf of St. Lawrence had been ordered closed to convoy traffic that month, and to many this seemed an admission of Canada's inability to stem the U-boat menace. Others felt it was a purely political decision rather than a military one, as the loss of such a number of ships would be of little consequence to the overall naval situation. As a result of the closing, shipments were sent by rail to Halifax and Saint John.

By the end of 1942, the U-boats withdrew from the Gulf of St. Lawrence, not to rest, but to avoid the increasing harassment of Canadian naval and air forces in the area, preferring to hunt once again the British-bound convoys departing New England's ports. But this time they were facing more escort ships and better-trained crews, equipped with new, often superior, assault weapons and much improved anti-sub detection equipment. Perhaps even more important was the growing number of patrol planes with modern radar. The amount of subs destroyed was growing, and so was the number of attacks and continued harassment on any U-boat which managed to surface, only to be driven off, damaged, or sunk. The tide was finally turning. The RCN had grown fifty-fold, and now, under scrutiny of new RCN Naval Rear-Admiral Leonard Murray, crews were receiving better training on more and better-equipped ships. As the RCN ships and crews now made up 48 percent of the Atlantic escorts, it was made clear that the RCN would make its own decisions and no longer automatically accept directives from the Royal Navy. The Royal Canadian Navy was coming into its own and was now capable of taking on U-boats.

But did Canada lose the Battle of the Gulf of St. Lawrence? Since 23 Allied ships were sunk in a relatively short period of time, and by a mere handful of German subs, of which none were destroyed, many critics thought it was a humiliating

*Destroyers and corvettes alongside #4 Jetty in Halifax, October 1942. One of the largest and busiest Canadian ports during the Second World War, Halifax's population swelled to three times its normal number.* (Library and Archives Canada PA-106063)

loss to Canada. A lack of sufficient escort support and training, as well as inefficient radar and ASDIC detection, contributed greatly to losses suffered. The Gulf of St. Lawrence must be considered a single, relatively small zone, and the battle for control of this area was ultimately won in the waters of the Atlantic. After all, 25,343 Allied crossings were made, 33 enemy subs were destroyed, and 165 million tons of vital supplies arrived safely.

### Fighting in the St. Lawrence

*I'm Jim Duthie and I served in the Navy from 1941 until 1945. And we went into the St. Lawrence because, at that time, the Germans were sinking a lot of boats in the St. Lawrence. So we went in there and had convoys come up and one particular one, in one particular convoy we had, there was five merchant ships and six RCN escort vessels, six of them. And the Germans sunk four of the five merchant ships that we had and one Canadian, one of the escort vessels. This particular time when the four of the five got sunk, they'd sink this one here and the other guys are coming along behind and they'd put down their boats and pick the guys up off of there and they'd just about, I've seen them there and they'd just get picked up and another torpedo would come and blow them in a lot of pieces."*

*Our captain, he was the boss of those six boats there. Whatever he said, well, that was it. He told all the rest of the escort vessels. And he just got kind of flustered there and he told everybody to just drop their depth charges, just keep dropping them. And this is the bad part. These guys were in the water. And the depth charges were too close to them, because the concussion you see, would just hurt them, not physically outside but in their insides it would hurt them. And we'd pick them up and bring them in and they'd still die because there didn't seem to be anything wrong with them except from the concussion. I can't remember that captain's name, I should have remembered it but anyhow, he got moved.*

*—Jim Duthie, Hartney, Manitoba,*
courtesy The Historica Memory Project

## HMCS *Spikenard*
*Flower Class corvette, torpedoed, February 11, 1942*

ON DECEMBER 8, 1941, THE HMCS *SPIKENARD*, NEWLY COMpleted out of the Davie Shipbuilding Co. at Lauzon, Quebec, received her commission. Originally destined, along with nine other corvettes, for use with the RN, the *Spikenard* was instead turned over to the Royal Canadian Navy. The 975-ton corvette was launched so late in the year that it had to break ice to get down the St. Lawrence on its way to Halifax. In January 1942, the *Spikenard* sailed as escort on a convoy to England, where it completed being fitted and underwent crew workups. So rushed was the demand for warships that HMCS *Spikenard* made the crossing without any heavy-gun armament. Instead it was fitted with a log, fashioned to resemble a 4-inch gun.

After spending the greater part of 1942 escorting convoys on the Iceland–UK run, the *Spikenard* was then sent back to St. John's, where it undertook a few weeks of anti-sub patrols before being re-assigned as an escort on the newly created Newfoundland–Londonderry route, nicknamed the "Newfy–Derry" run. The *Spikenard* was considered a good ship to serve on. The camaraderie came from the top, as all who served under the chief officer, Lieutenant-Commander Bert Shadforth, rated him second-to-none. His competence, fairness, and good sense of humour certainly was a factor in the *Spikenard* being considered a "happy" ship, and with the addition of fun-loving Lieutenant Charles Fawcett to the crew in January 1942, the ship became even more so.

Convoy SC-67 had left Halifax on January 30, picking up more ships at Sydney before heading east, just off the Grand Banks, to meet up with the corvette escorts, including the fleet command ship, the *Spikenard*. Little did SC-67 suspect that Kapitänleutnant Heinrich Zimmermann of U-136 was on the prowl on his first patrol. On February 5, five hundred kilometres west of Ireland, Zimmermann made his first kill, sinking escort corvette HMS *Arbutus* before continuing his search for fresh targets.

By February 10, SC-67 was eight hundred kilometres south of Iceland, making its way smoothly and steadily despite the black night and heavy seas. The corvettes *Louisburg, Dauphin, Chilliwack, Lethbridge*, and *Shediac* were in their proper positions, at least as well as the high seas would allow. The convoy was following the standard zigzag procedure at a relatively low speed since SC-67 was sailing as a "slow" convoy. Radio and radar contact was still very imprecise at this stage of the war as was ASDIC reliability, and the *Spikenard,* which was sailing at the front of the starboard column, was known to have inoperable radar during this convoy. By 2230 hours, U-136 had located the convoy, gotten in position, and quickly fired off a barrage of four bow torpedoes, striking the Norwegian carrier *Heina* and the *Spikenard* at almost the same time. The *Heina* managed to stay afloat for three hours, allowing all of its crew of thirty to be picked up safely. The *Spikenard*, hit between the bridge and foredeck and mortally wounded, drifted off into the darkness and sank within five minutes. The rest of the convoy, assuming the two explosions were from the *Heina*, did not notice the *Spikenard* was missing until eight hours later when it did not answer radio calls. It sunk so quickly, there had been no time for distress signals. All officers on the bridge were assumed to have been killed immediately, and any men in the water would have been killed by the secondary explosions from the boiler or depth charges, or eventually from exposure in the icy waters. Surprisingly at least eight crew members survived, after lying, soaked and half submerged, in a small rescue raft for what must have felt like an eternity, and were eventually picked up by corvette HMS *Gentian*.

Although the *"Spike"* is now long gone, it is still spoken of in affectionate terms by the depleted ranks of naval veterans, recalling the easygoing manner of its crew and beloved commander.

## HMCS *Raccoon*
### *Armed yacht, torpedoed and sunk, September 7, 1942*

BY SEPTEMBER 1942, GERMAN U-BOATS WERE ENTRENCHED in the fertile hunting grounds of the Gulf of St. Lawrence. Earlier in the month, several merchant ships had been sunk by German torpedoes, and the U-boat commanders, aware of the shortage of proper convoy escorts on the busy Quebec City–Sydney run, were in no hurry to finish their streak. By September 6, *U-165* was tracking QS-33, a small convoy of eight ships which had left Quebec a few days previously. Led by the Flower Class corvette HMCS *Arrowhead*, QS-33 was also being escorted by two fairmile motor launches, the minesweeper HMCS *Truro*, and the armed yacht HMCS *Raccoon*. Originally an American-owned luxury yacht, the *Raccoon* was one of sixteen yachts bought in 1940 to provide anti-submarine patrols and escort service, however minimal, to Canadian coastal convoys. Barely armed with one 3-inch gun and a depth charge-launcher, and with no radar, ASDIC, or even a radio phone, the *Raccoon* was severely limited in daytime communication and relied on signal, or Aldis, lamps. At night, when the threat of a U-boat attack was greatest, the *Raccoon* would be virtually helpless.

The RCAF did what it could in helping to protect the convoys and could be quite effective as U-boats considered airplanes their most serious threat. But with the heavy cloud cover, and especially fog, that was present on the night of September 6, the RCAF was brought to a standstill. At 2210 hours on September 6, U-165 launched a torpedo which found its target, slamming into the lead ship, the Greek freighter SS *Aeas*. Fortunately, although it went down quickly, only two of the *Aeas*'s crew of forty-one were lost.

The lead escort *Arrowhead* immediately went into action, firing star shells to illuminate the area in a vain attempt to locate the U-boat and pick up survivors. The *Raccoon*, which had been trailing the convoy, was last seen zigzagging, trying, it was assumed by the other ships, to find the sub. The armed yacht had already experienced a close call with an enemy sub a few days earlier when it spotted two torpedoes narrowly missing hitting the bow. At 0112 hours in the early morning of September 7, about three hours after the initial attack, the other convoy escorts heard explosions and noticed rising plumes of water. Once again it was thought that the *Raccoon* was in action, firing depth charges at the U-boat. The convoy made continuous attempts to contact the *Raccoon* but received only silence. Nothing more was found of the *Raccoon* until several days later when a bit of debris and the body of crewman Lieutenant R. H. McConnell was picked up. The HMCS *Raccoon* and its complete crew of thirty-seven were lost, including Lieutenant-Commander John Norman Smith. On the afternoon of September 7, convoy QS-33, now off Cap des Rosiers, came under attack once more as U-517, under the command of Paul Hartwig, released three lethal torpedoes with deadly accuracy, sinking three merchant ships.

The crew of U-165 did not have long to celebrate their grisly victory as the sub, on its way home on September 27, was sunk by a patrolling aircraft off the coast of France with the loss of all aboard, including the commander, Korvettenkapitän Eberhard Hoffmann.

The decimation of convoy QS-33 was heartbreaking, with the loss of four of its eight merchant ships, as well as the armed yacht *Raccoon*, making it the highest-percentage loss of any convoy thus far in the conflict.

Unfortunately, many more ships, both merchant and navy, would be lost before the RCN, by weight of experience, more arms and equipment, and especially ships and aircraft, would gain the upper hand in the struggle for control of the North Atlantic.

### HMCS *Charlottetown*
*Flower Class corvette, torpedoed and sunk September 11, 1942*

*"I went to breakfast and ordered two sausages. I got two torpedoes instead."*
—John Kinch, HMCS Charlottetown *survivor*

THE FLOWER CLASS CORVETTE HMCS *CHARLOTTETOWN* was one of 123 warships of this class eagerly awaited by the RCN for immediate escort duty on the hard-pressed Quebec–Sydney run. Built in Kingston, Ontario, the *Charlottetown* was in Halifax and fit for service by December 17, 1941. Outfitted with 2C Radar and type 127DV ASDIC, the *Charlottetown* carried thirty depth charges, two .303-calibre Lewis machine guns, as well as twin .50-calibre machine guns and a foredeck-mounted

BL 4-inch single gun. After serving well as part of the Western Local Escort Force out of Halifax, increased U-boat activities in the St. Lawrence sector eventually necessitated the transfer of the *Charlottetown* to the Gulf Escort Force.

Disaster awaited the *Charlottetown* on September 11, 1942. After completing a successful convoy run with SQ-30 to Rimouski, it was returning to base at Gaspé accompanied by the Bangor Class minesweeper HMCS *Clayoquot*. Because the *Clayoquot* was running low on fuel, both ships were sailing much slower than usual and were not using the standard zigzag running mode. Commander Paul Hartwig of U-517, who was in great part responsible for the SQ-33 debacle less than a week earlier, was lying in wait, allowing the two ships to come to him. At 0800 hours, he fired two torpedoes which struck the *Charlottetown* moments apart, shocking the residents of the tiny community who witnessed the tragic loss. At least one sailor was killed outright. As the heavily damaged ship went down in a mere four minutes, many were thrown or jumped into the frigid water. At least one lifeboat and two of the small carley floats were able to be launched and were soon filled.

In all, ten of the *Charlottetown*'s complement of sixty-four died as a result of the encounter. Included was Lieutenant-Commander John Bonner. Bonner had the depth charges set to a "safe" position before the ship went down, but there was a possible malfunction, because, as the ship was sinking, its depth charges detonated, killing five and severely wounding thirteen more of those still in the water. Lieutenant-Commander Bonner's body was recovered and tied temporarily to a piece of wreckage, but drifted away unnoticed and was never seen again. One frantic survivor, Leon-Paul Fortin, clung desperately to the side of a rescue vessel until he was finally hauled aboard to safety, seconds before he was ready to give up and let go. Another survivor, John Kinch, expressed the situation quite succinctly, saying, "I went to breakfast and asked for two sausages and got two torpedoes instead."

Survivors were brought to Gaspé for treatment of severe injuries and shock. One crew member, Tommy MacDonald, though severely wounded, tried to retrieve a float to help his buddies, but the effort worsened his wound and he died later in Gaspé, a true hero. Another seaman, John Garland, after helping his mates secure life jackets, was determined to go below to retrieve his beloved dog, Screech, who was the ship's mascot. Sadly, Garland did not survive the attempt. Screech, as it turned out, was already in safe hands. The beloved mascot was later presented by crew members to Garland's mother in a bittersweet ceremony a few weeks after the tragedy.

Though the *Clayoquot* went after *U-517* with everything at its disposal, Hartwig had once more gotten away cleanly. It would not be the last the RCN would see of that German sub.

### HMCS *Ottawa*
*Destroyer, torpedoed and sunk, September 13, 1942*

ORIGINALLY KNOWN AS THE HMS *CRUSADER*, THE *OTTAWA* already had over ten years of service when it was bought and renamed by the RCN in June 1938, and sent to serve on the west coast. When war broke out, the *Ottawa* was reassigned to Halifax for convoy duties between the UK and Canada, including escorting the 1ST Canadian Infantry Division to Britain. After suffering serious damage in a collision with a tugboat in 1940, the *Ottawa* underwent two months of repairs before being assigned again to escort duties for the 10TH Escort Group out of Greenock, Scotland. During that year, the *Ottawa* took part in the rescue of two merchant ship crews which had been destroyed by German U-boats. As well, along with the HMS *Harvester*, it took part in the sinking of the Italian sub *Comandante Faa Di Bruno*. Later, in November of 1940, it participated in the rescue of twenty-nine survivors of the grain carrier SS *Bussom*. By June 1941, U-boats were increasing their presence in the Western Atlantic sector, and the RCN assigned the *Ottawa* to the Newfoundland Escort Force, where, armed and with a capable crew and experienced commander, it was expected to be a vital addition to convoy protection. The U-boat wolfpacks actually did use wolf-like tactics of circling they prey, decoying, darting, and selecting the injured, lame, or slowest out of their midst, then disappearing quickly. And these wolfpacks were never above risking injury to themselves in their attacks.

Convoy ON-27 departed Liverpool on September 4, 1942, destined for North America. A day later, the convoy, consisting of 35 cargo freighters, met the RCN mid-ocean Escort Force Group C-4, consisting of 4 destroyers and 4 corvettes. There may have been plenty of firepower, but detection equipment was severely lacking. None of the escort ships had HF/DF direction finding sets, nor did any have operational 271-centimetre wavelength radar. Unknown to the fleet, the Kriegsmarine had successfully decoded the British Naval Cypher Number 3. Eight hundred kilometres off the coast of Ireland, just far enough to be safe from a land-based air attack, a wolfpack of no less than 13 U-boats was forming...and waiting.

Convoy ON-27 came under daytime attack on September 10, and further nighttime attacks on the 12th, 13th, and early hours of the 14th when the *Ottawa*, hit by two torpedoes, went to the bottom. By this time, six freighters had been sunk. Although three subs were damaged, all managed to get away safely. The escort ships did the best they could, but weak ASDIC contact, lack of radar, inability to find the targets, and mis-judgements left the cargo ships wide open to torpedoes. And the daring tactics of the U-boats made defence very difficult.

The *Ottawa* was last to be targeted, with one of four tor-pedoes fired making contact with the ship at 0105 hours. The wound was serious, and, although the boat was not sinking, it could not respond to manoeuvres correctly. A mere ten min-utes later, as the men undoubtedly were breathing a sigh of relief to be still afloat, a second torpedo struck, fatally break-ing the back of the *Ottawa*. Pandemonium reigned as the crew received the order to abandon ship, jumping into the water and scrambling for lifeboats or anything that floated. Luckily, other ships were quickly on the scene to pick up survivors. Sixty-nine of the *Ottawa*'s crew were plucked safely out of the freezing water. Sadly, the total of those lost numbered 114, including Lieutenant-Commander Clark Anderson Rutherford. In hon-our of the *Ottawa*, at least three other warships launched since its demise have been named HMCS *Ottawa*.

## ss *Caribou*
### *Marine ferry, torpedoed and sunk, October 14, 1942*

TECHNICALLY, THE *CARIBOU* WAS NOT CLASSIFIED AS AN Allied ship of war, although on the day of the vessel's demise there were 118 military personnel on board. And the ferry did sail with an escort. This, in the mind of U-69's skipper, Kapitänleutnant Ulrich Graf, made the *Caribou* a fair target.

The *Caribou* was a large, hulking vessel displacing almost 3,600 tons. Unfortunately, it was also a sitting duck for U-boat attacks. The German subs had been decimating Allied ship-ping in the Gulf of St. Lawrence, attacking seven convoys and sinking twenty-two merchant ships over the previous eight months. On the night of October 14, the *Caribou* was nearing the end of its journey, escorted by the minesweeper *Grandmere*. The commander of the *Grandmere* was none too happy to see all the smoke belching from the *Caribou*'s funnel, nor did he feel being assigned to the ferry's rear position was as effective as picking up a U-boat on radar in front of the *Caribou*.

U-69 was, in fact, lying just ahead in the *Caribou*'s path. Kapitan Graf took his time, firing only one torpedo, hitting the *Caribou* on its starboard side. The damage was massive. Many of the floats and lifeboats were too damaged to use. Chaos was rampant as the ferry went down in six minutes. Separated families sought to find each other, but most could do nothing, hardly having time to jump overboard themselves into the ice-cold Atlantic waters.

HMCS *Grandmere* went into action stations immediately, and its crew spotted and quickly tried to ram U-69. Meanwhile, Graf headed for safety beneath the *Caribou*'s debris, where his sub was not noticed, and he knew it would not likely be attacked, since people from the *Caribou* were still in that area. U-69 was able to leave the area a few hours later when all was much quieter.

The losses were heartbreaking. Of the 11 children on board, only 1, 15-month-old Leonard Shiers, survived. The 46-man crew was decimated, with 31 lost. At least 5 families were virtually wiped out. In total, 137 people were lost.

# 1943

IN 1943, REAR-ADMIRAL MURRAY BECAME COMMANDER-in-Chief, Canadian Northwest Atlantic, the only Canadian chosen to command an Allied theatre of operations in the Second World War. Further, the training and equipment problems were being overcome. Specialist schools in signalling, radar, and ASDIC were now pumping out scores of well-trained young men to meet the pace of rapidly changing weapon and detection technology. With more ships coming online, convoys were now being escorted by carrier groups trained in search and attack methods. As the RCN's strength grew, RN ships left to fight in other areas. Within another year, the whole of the North Atlantic would be under jurisdiction of the RCN.

By late 1943, Admiral Doenitz knew the tide had turned and stated, "We have lost the Battle of the Atlantic."

### HMCS *Louisburg*
*Flower Class corvette, sunk by aircraft, February 6, 1943*

*"You know, I'm not too religious. When the ship was going down, it's amazing how religious you get all of a sudden."*
—*Ernie Pain, interview* Standard Freeholder,
November 11, 2010

OPERATING IN PROXIMITY TO ENEMY AIR BASES ADDED a serious concern for warships, as there was the additional threat of coming under attack by enemy aircraft, as happened to convoy KMF-8. That particular incident resulted in the loss of the HMCS *Louisburg* and forty-one men of its full complement of eighty-four crew members. The *Louisburg*, a Flower Class corvette built in Quebec City and sailing under the command of Lieutenant-Commander William Franklin Campbell, RCNVR, had served well on convoy escort duty since its commission in October 1941.

On February 6, 1943, at 1915 hours, and approximately one hundred kilometres northeast of Oran in the Mediterranean Sea, KMF-8 came under attack by two separate formations of seven enemy bombers and seven torpedo-carrying planes. The *Louisburg* and its fellow escorts, the *Prescott, Regina, Woodstock, Algoma,* and *Laforey,* immediately went into action positions. All Oerlikon anti-aircraft guns opened up, downing at least two torpedo bombers. An aerial torpedo barely missed the *Laforey*, and the freighter *Fort Babine* had already been hit and seriously damaged. Torpedo planes were coming in on the *Louisburg* fast and so low that the *Louisburg* had to stop firing lest it hit the *Woodstock*, directly in front of her guns. To make matters much more difficult, the planes were coming in with the sun at their back, severely restricting the *Louisburg*'s field of vision. At 1920 hours, only five minutes into the attack, tragedy struck the *Louisburg* as the ship took a torpedo bomb to its port side.

Seaman Ernie Pain survived the explosion, and despite being knocked out cold, he recalls the captain giving the frantic orders to abandon ship. "You know, I'm not too religious. When the ship was going down, it's amazing how religious you get all of a sudden," he says. Pain quickly grabbed a life jacket and headed for the water where he joined those who were making for the lifeboats. The ship went down in four minutes with several of the crew already dead or trapped inside. Commander Campbell decided at the last moment to go below to see that nobody was left behind, but within seconds, at 1924 hours, the ship began its final plunge. The difficulty in releasing carley floats and life rafts within that short time span undoubtedly added to the death toll, as did the explosion of some of the depth charges. Even after being picked up by the HMS *Lookout*, the danger was not over for the survivors. "We were put on the mess deck, and aircraft were still trying to bomb the ship we were on. It was not very nice," recalls Pain. "Fifty-six men were sent to the hospital, some were sent to the morgue."

As well as being honoured for a substantial contribution to the war effort, the HMCS *Louisburg* can claim the distinction of being the only Canadian warship to be sunk by an enemy aircraft.

## HMCS *Weyburn*
*Flower Class corvette, hit mine and sunk, February 22, 1943*

BUILT IN PORT ARTHUR IN 1941, THE HMCS *WEYBURN*, one of the early Flower Class corvettes, was commissioned and ready for service by November 1941. Over the next two years, the *Weyburn* was active in Atlantic convoy escort and anti-submarine duties. In several cases, it was able to pick up survivors from stricken cargo vessels, rescuing forty-two men from the merchant ship *Fredricka Lensen*, which had been heavily damaged by a torpedo from U-132 on July 20, 1942, and three crew members from the oil tanker *Athelsultan*, which had been sunk by U-617 on September 23, 1942.

On February 22, 1943, the *Weyburn* was cruising near Gibraltar, under command of Acting-Lieutenant-Commander Thomas Maitland Wake Goldby, RCNR. Goldby was unaware that the area had recently been seeded with sixty-six mines by U-118. The *Weyburn*, having just finished refuelling, was returning to its screening position with convoy MKS-8, when it struck a mine and suffered extensive damage. The ship immediately settled at the stern and began sinking. The convoy escort, destroyer HMS *Wivern*, came alongside immediately, taking on thirty-one ratings and officers. Crew members rushed desperately to disable depth charge primers, but when the *Weyburn* finally went down, two of the depth charges went off, killing and injuring several men in the water. The HMCS *Wivern*, standing off a short distance, was severely damaged and had to be taken under tow by the RN sloop *Black Swan*. The tragic loss of the *Weyburn* included twelve men and it is considered fortunate that seventy-one men survived the ordeal.

Several acts of bravery and courage occurred that fatal night as men from both ships tried frantically to help their crewmates. The commander of the *Weyburn*, Tom Golby, though suffering from a massive head injury and in a daze, continued to aid his men until he met his fate. Wilfred Beck from Montreal and Ordinary Seaman Stoker Frank Day, a *Wivern* crew member, also lost their lives while helping others. Lieutenant-Commander William Garrard suffered severe, crushing damage to his ankle while attempting to disarm the depth charges. He was rescued, but it was determined that his

*Able Seaman Daniel Ralph of Esquimalt, British Columbia, with the mascot of the patrol vessel* Allaverdi *in November 1941. Seamen took their pets seriously. In fact, one young sailor lost his life when he remained aboard a sinking ship to look for his beloved dog. The pooch survived.* (Library and Archives Canada PA-134093)

injured foot would have to be amputated. Garrard's reply of "Hack away, boys. I'm in favour of it," became famous among his peers.

Stoker Thomas Baxter, of Penetanguishene, Ontario, carried the *Weyburn*'s mascot, a little springer spaniel called Posh, off the sinking ship. Posh had swallowed a lot of oil and wasn't doing too well, but managed to survive and was sent back home to Canada to its original owner Pam Golby. Pam was the five-year-old daughter of the *Weyburn*'s commander Tom Golby, who insisted that her dad take Posh along with him when he went off to serve his country. Mascots, mostly dogs, were carried on many RCN warships. Perhaps because a pet was a common denominator among the crew, considering the various personalities aboard, the pooches, or sometimes cats, were respected and enjoyed by all.

## HMCS *St. Croix*
*Destroyer, torpedoed and sunk, September 20, 1943*

*No one in the boats died during the night, it was morning that everything happened. Men on the carley floats insisted on getting into the rowboat. As the men got in, it settled lower in the water. Just before the rescue ship came along, it sank. The whaler did not have any injured men aboard. They were oil-grimed and cold. I saw men who were tough, big men. They hung out all night in the hope a boat would pick them up. Then when the boat did not come into view they died. I guess they couldn't hang out any longer. We dropped them into the sea.*

—*William Allan Fisher, survivor*

ORIGINALLY BUILT IN 1919 FOR THE UNITED STATES NAVY as USS *McCook,* the venerable old destroyer was in the naval reserve and nearly out to pasture when, in 1939, it was recommissioned for duty in the US Atlantic Fleet. In 1940, the *McCook* was transferred to the RN as part of a fifty-warship swap with Britain in return for US air and naval bases on Canadian and British soil. Later in the year, it was renamed the HMCS *St. Croix* and transferred, along with five other aging destroyers, to the RCN for escort duty, after having arms and equipment sufficiently upgraded. On its first run, to the UK, the *St. Croix* faced a massive hurricane and had to return to Halifax where it was laid up for three months to undergo major repairs. Over the next two years, the warship served well as escort on various convoy runs, recording notable successes against enemy U-boats, having sunk *U-90* on July 24,

*Destoyers bristled with deck guns of all sizes, including Bofors, Oerlikon, and pom-pom guns, as well as heavy four-inch barrage guns.* (Library and Archives Canada PA-105277)

1942, and assisting the corvette HMCS *Sackville* in sinking *U-87* on March 4, 1943.

In September 1943, the *St. Croix* found itself in the Bay of Biscay on patrol as a part of a hunter-killer group which also included the corvettes *Morden, Chambly, Sackville*, the destroyer *St. Francis*, and the RN frigate HMS *Itchen*. Keeping a protective eye on two convoys, ONS-18 and ON-202, the crew of the *St. Croix* and their cohorts couldn't help but feel nervous as they were well aware of the late summer resurgence of U-boat attacks. The Kriegsmarine was eager to use its newly developed Gnat (German Naval Acoustic Torpedo), which was designed to home in on the sounds of a ship's propeller.

By September 16, a large U-boat wolfpack had found both convoys, and a running battle was soon underway. The HMCS *St. Croix* and its group were quickly ordered to speed to the convoys where more protection was desperately needed.

On September 20, coming up astern of ONS-18, Lieutenant-Commander A. H. Dobson was aware that several U-boat sightings were made earlier in the day, and enemy attacks had already been foiled with at least one going down to an RAF Liberator torpedo. Everything seemed quiet at the moment, but that was about to change as Kapitänleutnant Rudolph Bahr of *U-338*, peering intently through his periscope, could hardly miss the *St. Croix* sail directly into his view.

Quickly, a Gnat torpedo was unleashed, finding its mark perfectly as the deadly charge exploded, obliterating the *St. Croix*'s stern. The ship stayed afloat, at least for a while. Commander Dobson coolly assessed the situation, and as his crew tried to keep the ship above water, he ordered the lifeboats out as a precaution. Just as Commander Dobson was satisfied that all his crew were in lifeboats, he signalled that he was "leaving the office." But *U-305* was not finished yet. Not wasting a Gnat torpedo, Bahr fired a standard torpedo at the *St. Croix*'s midsection, effectively cutting her in two. Able Seaman William Allan Fisher, the lone survivor of the *St. Croix* sinking, tells of his experiences.

*We were part of an escort detailed to a large convoy, and we received a signal that submarines were about. We stayed astern of the convoy, but on September 20, we had to come up and take on oil from a tanker in the convoy. On our way back to our position we saw a Canadian four-motored liberator signalling us. We were told that they had spotted a submarine and dropped depth charges. We flashed two boilers and made for the spot at twenty-four knots. As we neared, we had to reduce speed. As we slowed up we were hit in the screws. There was no panic and no one thought of abandoning ship, but in two minutes another torpedo struck, this time near the mess deck, and water began to pour in. The captain, Lieutenant Commander Dobson, then issued orders to abandon ship. That was just before 8 o'clock and dusk.*

Some men were injured by the explosions which followed the torpedoes, some were burned and cut. They were put in the motor launch before it was lowered over the side. The launch pulled away. Meanwhile, attempts were made to lower a sixty-passenger oar-driven whaler. Two attempts resulted in two large holes being gouged into the bottom of the whaler. Carley floats were dumped over the side and the men began jumping into the water. "No one seemed worried then," Fisher relates. "Many of the crew laughed that they would be due for twenty-nine-day survivor's leave." The rowboat pulled away from the sinking destroyer and picked men out of the water. "Even then I thought the ship would be saved. Then I saw the captain dive off the boat. I knew everyone was off then and that the captain had given up hope.

"As Lieutenant Commander Dobson headed for the motor boat, he saw two men struggling in the water. He towed them to carley floats and then made for the rowboat. I was in charge of the motor boat. Sixty men were still alive on the whaler."

The ship which headed to their rescue was the Royal Navy frigate *Itchen*. As the frigate steamed through the lifting morning mist, the men in the whaler received the signal that the *Itchen* would come directly to their rescue.

Kapitan Bahr, still lurking, could not believe his luck and quickly fired a Gnat at the looming *Itchen*. Perhaps it was the *Itchen*'s speed, but it managed to outrace or perhaps outmanoeuvre the Gnat, which exploded in the frigate's wake. But this was enough to shake up the *Itchen* which then decided it would be wiser to wait for the arrival of the corvette HMS *Polyanthus* before picking up survivors, a very dangerous procedure to attempt alone, especially with the lurking U-305. Firing star shells to help a rescue boat find survivors was also standard procedure, but in this case attracted at least four more U-boats to the scene. As the *Polyanthus* fended off one of these lethal predators, another enemy sub simply took aim, firing a Gnat that sunk the ship and its entire crew, save for a few survivors. "The *Polyanthus* was just coming in and she was struck," Fisher says. "I guess she went down in about ten minutes. We rescued ten men in our whaler." It was becoming a massacre. The *Itchen* could not get to the men that night as it was involved in either chasing down the attacking U-boats or fending them off. The following morning, it was able to pick up eighty-one very relieved survivors from the *St. Croix* and one from the *Polyanthus*. Sadly, those plucked out of the frigid Atlantic waters would have only a brief respite as later in the day of September 22, time ran out for the *Itchen* as it was hit one again.

Fisher goes on:

*Some of us were given jobs to do. I did watch. On September 22, two days after we were rescued, we were ordered to our action stations because submarines were around. We had three orders. The first started at 6 at night. There was another one at 7 and again at 9. At 9 o'clock I was standing beside the funnel when a torpedo struck. I was knocked thirty feet and landed against a gun platform. As I crawled toward the rail I kept yelling for my pal, Stoker Rod MacKenzie, of Sydney. MacKenzie had been torpedoed six times before. He didn't answer and I jumped over the side. As I hit the water there was another explosion and I felt that my stomach was being squeezed through my ears. They just cracked.*

When Fisher reached down to tug off his boots, the left one was missing. It had been blown off. Fisher grabbed aboard and looked to see other men jumping from the ship. Most of them drowned. A carley float drifted by and Fisher jumped on. During the night others jumped on, but most of them died.

Only two of the *Itchen*'s crew survived, and sadly only one of the *St. Croix*'s eighty-one original survivors was rescued. The three survivors were eventually picked up by the Polish freighter *Wisla*.

The concentrated U-boat attack on convoys ON-18 and ON-202 clearly shows what the RCN was up against as the Battle of the Atlantic raged. That is, an unseen enemy, innovative and determined, using state-of-the-art weaponry. Eventually, with precise Allied planning and detection methods, the U-boat wolfpacks would be so challenged, harassed, and pressured that their effectiveness was reduced to a much lesser threat.

Fisher's account, from the *Winnipeg Free Press*, October 1, 1943, of loss and survival exemplifies the inherent dangers of naval warfare against a formidable enemy.

### HMCS *Chedabucto*
*Bangor Class minesweeper,*
*sunk in collision, September 21, 1943*

THE SINKING OF THE HMCS *CHEDABUCTO* MARKED THE sixth and last loss of a RCN warship due to marine accidents and/or storm conditions. Previously the destroyers HMCS *Fraser* and *Margaree*, the armed trawler *Bras D'or*, the armed yacht *Otter*, and Flower Class corvette HMCS *Windflower* were lost in circumstances other than direct enemy action. At first glance this number may seem high, but it must be taken into account that the last accident occurred in 1943, long before the end of the war, which suggests that lack of experienced and trained personnel was a large factor in these early tragedies. But, considering the volatility of the North Atlantic, and the number of ships sailing in convoy, as well as the difficulty in recruiting experienced and reliable officers in the early years, the number is not overly surprising.

The Bangor Class minesweeper *Chedabucto* was built and commissioned at Esquimalt on the British Columbian coast in 1941, and was sent to Halifax for escort duty in December of 1941. On April 10, 1942, the *Chedabucto* was tasked with towing a safe distance offshore and sink the British freighter SS *Trongate*, which had caught fire in Halifax Harbour with a cargo of explosives aboard. In June 1942, the *Chedabucto* was transferred to convoy air/sea duty on the Quebec–Sydney run. Following a lengthy refit in Lunenburg in 1943, it was then assigned to the Gaspé force. On the night of October 21, 1943, the *Chedabucto* found itself on the St. Lawrence River about fifty kilometres from Rimouski, Quebec, assigned to short escort duty for the British cable ship *Lord Kelvin*. Having escorted the *Lord Kelvin* to Rimouski, the *Chedabucto* was patrolling while waiting for her next assignment, which was to escort the *Citadella*, a small fire tug, to its proper convoy.

It was a clear night, visibility good at about ten kilometres. Sub-Lieutenant J. R. Morrison had the early 0400–0800-hours watch. Morrison was not yet a certified watch-keeper but, despite Captain J. H. B. Davies's efforts to secure qualified personnel, none had yet been forthcoming. By 0520 hours, everything on the watch was recorded as fine. Radar monitoring in several nearby ships noticed nothing amiss. At 0540 hours, the *Lord Kelvin* materialized seemingly out of nowhere, and before there was any chance at all to react, embedded itself deeply into the *Chedabucto*. The *Lord Kelvin* backed out of the wound quickly, a manoeuvre which would only worsen the situation, allowing seawater to flood the *Chedabucto* and causing it to list quickly to ten degrees. But the ship was still afloat, and despite difficulties in slowing the flooding, was, once the crew was removed, taken under tow by the uss *Buttonwood*, heading for Rimouski. It soon was apparent that the ship would go down before they reached Rimouski, so the *Buttonwood* headed instead for the beaches off Bic Island. A kilometre or so offshore, the *Chedabucto* gave up its ghost, quickly rolled over, and went down. Fortunately, since the ship carried a full complement of eighty-three men, only one was killed in the collision, Sub-Lieutenant (Engineer) D. W. Tuke, RCNVR.

Inquiry results held that severe censure and displeasure be directed at the captain of the *Chedabucto*, who, the inquiry concluded, was responsible for leaving an unqualified officer in charge on the bridge. But for Captain Davies, the inquiry findings could have been worse as Naval Headquarters in

Ottawa recommended a full court martial. The final decision rested on Admiral Leonard W. Murray, who didn't think the incident warranted more than an official entry of "severe displeasure," recorded in Davies's service files. The whole affair was finally over, save for Western Union's demand that they be compensated for time lost during the extensive repairs needed to make the *Lord Kelvin* seaworthy once again.

# 1944

THE BATTLE OF THE ATLANTIC WAS ULTIMATELY decided over a two-month period with the introduction and implementation of a variety of technologically superior equipment combined with a massive increase in the number of Allied warships, especially those trained and equipped for hunt-and-destroy tactics. U-boats were now coming away from convoy battles with their noses bloodied. In the past encounters, where an eight-sub wolfpack would lose perhaps one sub, they were now losing eight out of ten. And the pressure was increasing. U-boats had to surface often to recharge batteries, and by 1944, due to Allied detection and immediate attack co-ordination measures, the RCN was able to pounce on subs as soon as they were spotted. This was no longer like the first few years. The RCN's ships were numerous, its crews now experienced and well trained.

In desperation, Doenitz tried new tactics and introduced the schnorkle, an extended tube-like device which enabled a sub to travel just below the surface, undetected as it sucked in the air needed to run its diesel engines. U-boats could now cover much longer distances undetected, so once again Doenitz sent his search-and-destroy patrols deep into Canadian waters. As a result, RCN warships took their heaviest losses in 1944, losing seven warships. Despite these losses, convoys were getting through in greater numbers, and U-boat losses were growing quickly. Doenitz's new tactic of equipping his boats with much heavier anti-aircraft guns in an attempt to ward off the ever-increasing torpedo-carrying attack planes did not work as he had hoped: the Liberators and Sunderlands simply retreated to just out of firing range while they radioed the sub's position to the nearest sub-hunters. If the U-boat went into a dive, it had a window of perhaps forty-five seconds to escape successfully before the Sunderland or Liberator would be upon it. The new German METOX radar did not work out as planned because, unknowingly, weak signals were emitted, enabling Coastal Command to detect a vessel's location.

### HMCS *Athabaskan*
*Destroyer, sunk by plane torpedo, April 29, 1944*

ALTHOUGH ONLY COMMISSIONED FOR DUTY IN 1943, the Tribal Class destroyer *Athabaskan* was already a battle-scarred and war-hardened veteran of naval warfare by April 29, 1944. While still in its construction berth in Newcastle-on-Tyne, England, the ship was bombed in a German air raid. It also suffered significant storm damage to its hull on one patrol and was involved in a collision with the HMS *Bargate* near Scapa Flow. In 1943, the *Athabaskan* made at least five trips to the Bay of Biscay and Gibraltar area, taking part in various patrol, escort, and U-boat hunting duties, as well as rescue operations.

Ordinary Seaman Andre Audet, who joined the RCN in Montreal in 1942, was assigned to the crew of the *Athabaskan* in 1943, and was on board when the vessel had a run-in with five German Dornier aircrafts. On that day of August 27, 1944, twenty of these Glider-Bombers had attacked a Canadian/ British support group on patrol near Gibraltar. Audet recalled the intense anti-aircraft fire as the battle merged. One of the new "flying torpedoes" unleashed by the Dorniers found its mark, slamming into the port side of the *Athabaskan*, just aft of the bridge. Luckily, the torpedo did not explode, but continued on straight through the ship and exited through the starboard bow where it finally exploded about six metres away. But as can be imagined, there was a lot of damage to the interior as the four-metre projectile destroyed the central control system for the guns and severely damaged the radar and communications system, Audet recalls. Five men were killed that day and twelve others seriously injured.

One survivor of that attack, Stuart Kettles, recalls, "As it went out the other side, the fins sheared off a Signalman's feet at the ankles. He stayed conscious long enough to apply tourniquets on himself. His name was Charles Kent and he was from Calgary."

As the crew struggled to put out fires, plug the many holes in the hull, and stop the numerous leaks, Captain G. A. Miles got the guns firing once more and re-entered the fray since the attack, which had hit and sunk the HMS *Egret*, was still ongoing. Finally the *Athabaskan* was able to limp back to base at Plymouth for repairs. Captain Miles chose their home port rather than the much closer docks at Gibraltar, knowing that repairs could be completed much faster at the huge British base. For, despite the near sinking, the crew and officers of the *Athabaskan* were eager to avenge their losses and were prepared to take another crack at the German Kriegsmarine.

Three months later, workups completed and with a new commander, Lieutenant-Commander John Stubbs, the *Athabaskan* was fit to go. By December 1943, the destroyer found itself accompanying three other Tribal Class warships, the *Iroquois, Huron,* and *Haida,* as they encountered the German cruiser *Scharnhors*t off North Cape. All four destroyers took part in the ensuing battle as the HMS *Duke of York* sunk the *Scharnhorst.*

By April 1944, the *Athabaskan,* as part of D-Day preparations, was assigned, along with the 10TH Destroyer Flotilla, to seek, harass, and destroy enemy operations in the English Channel and off the coast of France. On April 26, Andre Audet, who now was a 20-millimetre Twin Mounted Oerlikon gunner, was again eyewitness to destruction as the *Athabaskan* combined with its sister ship, the *Haida,* in a close-up manoeuvre and pounded the German Destroyer *T-29* until it sank. Two other German Destroyers, the *T-24* and *T-27,* no doubt looking for RCN warships to avenge the *T-29,* were intercepted around 0400 hours on April 29. Star shells lit up the night sky as the battle joined, the firing heavy from both quarters. Smoke was laid down by both Canadian destroyers as they turned away, presenting a narrower, much smaller target. The two German destroyers did the same, but as they did, each fired six torpedoes. The *Haida* was not touched, but at least one torpedo from the deadly volley penetrated the *Athabaskan*'s stern and exploded. Survivor Gerry Webster recalls the chaos which followed: "They hit our stern with a torpedo and blew it away. We were like sitting ducks and the next torpedo hit us amidships. There were fires everywhere. Oil was shooting in the air and we got the call to abandon ship."

Able Seaman Harry Liznick, a gunner on the *Athabaskan* at the time, also recalls the event: "I could see flames everywhere shooting one-hundred feet into the air, as well as hanging pipes, chunks of steel and iron. I thought to myself that all this steel will kill me if it came down." Burned about his face and fearing for his life, Liznick jumped overboard and swam for all his worth. Safely away from the crippled ship, the young seaman "watched as the stern went under and the bow came up and the good old *Athabaskan* slid under and sank at 0442. Those trapped below deck went down with the ship."

Andre Audet also found himself swimming for his life, barely hanging on to some floats from a fishing net. He made it to a small motor launch which held five others, and later a larger launch from the *Haida* picked them up. Audet's ordeal was over. One hundred and twenty-eight crew members were killed or lost at sea. German warships picked up eighty-five men, who were sent to German prison camps. Another forty-eight men survived the ordeal, most having been picked up by the *Haida*.

There were many acts of heroism that night. Lieutenant-Commander Stubbs, bleeding and severely burnt, had joined his men in the frigid waters, trying to keep their spirits up by leading them in song and exhorting them to keep their limbs moving until help arrived. Unfortunately Stubbs, like so many others, succumbed to the cold. At one point, Stubbs could have been picked up by the *Haida*, but refused as he continued to swim and help his men into rescue boats. For his unselfish actions, the genial commander of the *Athabaskan* was awarded the Distinguished Service Cross posthumously. The HMCS *Athabaskan* is now enshrined in history as the only RCN warship to be lost in action against enemy surface ships.

### HMCS *Valleyfield*
*River Class frigate, torpedoed and sunk, May 7, 1944*

AS A RIVER CLASS FRIGATE BUILT IN QUEBEC CITY IN 1943, the *Valleyfield* was a relatively new ship in the fast-growing Canadian fleet, although it had already gained valuable experience on the overseas convoy route. By May 1944, the *Valleyfield* was nearing completion of its second overseas escort assignment, having handed off the charges to another escort group, and was heading for its home port of St. John's. The U-boat threat on the convoy routes was considered much lessened as, with the massive buildup in the English Channel area by Allied warships in preparation for the coming invasion, the German Kriegsmarine was recalling many of its subs to bolster defence. The Germans knew that if France were lost, so too would the all-important naval bases in the occupied country. However, on May 1, 1944, a U-boat was sighted east of Conception Bay and was attacked by a Liberator aircraft. Firing from both sides ensued, but the sub managed to escape. Over the next several days, U-548, under command of Kapitan Heinrich Zimmermann, was hunted by the HMS *Hargood* without success.

On the night of May 7, the *Valleyfield*, accompanied by two other frigates and two corvettes, was about eighty kilometres south of Cape Race, nearing home and cruising smoothly. Suddenly, the *Valleyfield*'s ASDIC sounded, detecting the presence of a U-boat. Action stations were sounded immediately. At the same time, torpedoes were sighted heading straight for the *Valleyfield*. U-548's Kapitan Zimmermann had come across the *Valleyfield* accidentally, and not believing his good luck, unhurriedly took careful aim and unleashed two deadly Gnat acoustic torpedoes. At least one of the lethal projectiles tore into the mid-ship port side of the vessel where the boilers were, causing a massive explosion to erupt, breaking the *Valleyfield*'s back. Chaos and mayhem quickly followed as the stricken frigate settled in the water. Within five minutes the ship went down. Those who were not killed outright by the blast were thrown or jumped into the frigid seas, many without life jackets, grabbing anything to stay afloat. Crew members were severely wounded, soaked, and choking on thick oil. The attack and sinking happened so quickly that it was thirty minutes before any of the other ships realized the *Valleyfield* was missing. Finally the HMCS *Giffard* realized what had happened and rushed to the scene to pick up survivors. But procedure called for the rescue ship to first clear the area of any submarine threat, so the *Giffard* had to leave the scene to make a sweep of the area. Meanwhile the *Giffard*'s captain contacted the remaining three ships to hunt for the U-boat while he returned to the *Valleyfield* site to pick up survivors. The water was zero degrees Celcius, and the men were weakening fast. The numbing cold was just too much as they perished by the dozen.

Robert Pickering of Chatham, Ontario, was a crew member aboard the rescue ship *Giffard* that night and recalls the sinking and rescue attempt:

> *And about 10 minutes after 12:00, there was a big boom and we thought that they were just practicing dropping depth charges and that, but we soon found out a torpedo had hit the [HMCS] Valleyfield on the left hand side. We were only half a mile astern of her. So we stopped and then the skipper realized that he shouldn't have stopped; and he took off again and made a swing around, see if they could get a [ASDIC] ping off of the submarine. And when he couldn't do that, there was three other ships there. He called them up to come back and hunt for the submarine. And we went back to pick up the survivors that we could find.* (The Historica Memory Project)

Of the 165 men who were aboard the *Valleyfield* that night, 127 were lost, including the ship's commander, D. T. English, and all but 2 of his officers. The loss of the HMCS *Valleyfield* was eventually recorded as the only RCN frigate in the Second World War to be sunk by enemy forces.

## MTB 460
*Sunk by mine, July 2, 1944*

AS PART OF THE 29TH MOTOR TORPEDO BOAT FLOTILLA, MTB 460 was only one of many who were given one of the most dangerous tasks of the war at sea. Using daring, speed, and stealth, these little coastal boats, bristling with weapons, would penetrate protected zones and take on warships of any size. The men aboard these MTBs were volunteers who knew and respected the harsh living conditions and the dangers involved. The basic crew generally consisted of their captain, first lieutenant, coxwain, leading stoker, able-seaman stoker, able-seaman gunner, a telegraphist, stoker, and an ordinary seaman (trained). Skirting over minefields at enemy port entrances was everyday work and the threat of oblivion was always near.

It happened without warning. On the night of July 2, 1944, crews on both MTB 460 and 465 were on the return home from a regular night patrol. All of a sudden a sheet of flame shot straight up from the 460's position followed by a column of water and debris. The men of the following MTB 465 did not need to be told what had happened as they dove for cover from the flying remains. The MTB 460 had hit a mine powerful enough to sink a destroyer, so it has to be considered fortunate that even six of the crew of sixteen survived. The commander of MTB 460, Lieutenant D. Killam, DSC, was lost along with nine of his men.

## MTB 463
*Sunk by mine, July 7, 1944*

ON THE NIGHT OF JULY 7, 1944, MTB 463, ALONG WITH MTB 466, was working the shoreline near Ouistrehan Canal sweeping and setting off small German mines. Twenty-six of these mines had already been successfully destroyed when disaster struck. MTB 463 suffered severe hole damage to its hull and began to settle.

Luckily, the mine was small and, although the 463 could not be saved, only four crew members and one officer were injured. The MTB 466, following closely behind, was able to pick up all survivors and bring the injured to a Polish destroyer which was anchored nearby. It was a close call for the crew. If the mine had been larger it could have been much more devastating. But the unheralded crews of the small 29TH Flotilla continued to work among the danger and daily threat of sudden death, unperturbed in their dedication and devotion to duty.

## HMCS *Regina*
*Corvette, torpedoed and sunk, August 8, 1944*

THE NEED FOR MORE FIGHTING SHIPS WAS STILL PRESSing in 1942. In fact, on the very day the HMCS *Regina* was commissioned, January 22, 1942, German U-boats sunk four more Canadian merchant ships in Canadian waters. By April, with the *Regina's* final fitting complete, it was ready for work, albeit with many green crew members and officers aboard. Jim Hawley recalls his bout with seasickness as a new recruit on the *Regina*:

> Some got really seasick. I felt sorry for the poor bastards, it was terrible I guess. The only thing I ever had was a headache and that was the first time going out Halifax harbour. And we were just going out, starting to go out where the big rocks are before you go out into the open sea. And we were just closing the portholes and scuttles, getting ready for sea. And

*I looked out and you could see the ground going up and down and I got a hell of a headache. And I remember an old Chief, he was sitting on the mess deck with me and I guess I looked pretty tepid and he said, "you're not feeling very good." He says, "go into the heads [toilet], put your finger down your throat and bring her up" and he said, you'll be fine. So I went into the heads and brought everything up and I never was seasick after that.* (The Historica Memory Project)

But the young men of the *Regina* gained experience fast, working with convoys in the Atlantic runs, the Mediterranean, the North Africa landings, the English Channel, and taking part, before and after, in D-Day operations. The *Regina* also participated in survivor rescue and the sinking of the Italian sub *Avorio.*

John Potter from Toronto also served on the *Regina* and describes his experiences aboard the ship:

*Well, the [HMCS] Regina was my first ship and I developed a love for it I think. The skipper of the Regina was a marvellous, marvellous man, Lieutenant-Commander Freeland. And he was, oh, the fellows would have gone anywhere with him. You more or less learnt on the job. None of the officers were, they were just brand spanking new, they never seen the ocean before in their life and maybe we had, I think we had two officers that were, had been to sea before and that was the skipper and a navigator. And that was it. All the rest were brand new, out of the officer's school. And the same with the, all those recruits. You know, we were just green as grass.*

*Not everybody was brand new. I'm sorry about that but fellows that had been moved from other ships to help train us and so on. And also, there were some RCN people. The coxswain was RCN and so on. And there was a few RCN people that were aboard with us. And they were more or less to help train us as we went. But you can imagine our first trip out, darned near everybody and his brother was all seasick, a terrible, terrible trip going to Saint Margaret Bay. (The Evening Telegram, May 25, 1943)*

In August of 1944, the *Regina* found itself plying the Wales–Normandy convoy routes under command of Lieutenant J. W. Radford, RCNR. On August 8 the corvette, the sole escort of convoy EBC-66, was just a few kilometres off Cornwall, England, heading for the Normandy beachhead when one of the cargo ships in her charge, the heavily laden US ship *Ezra Weston*, struck what the merchant ship's captain reported was a mine, with heavy damage ensuing. Taking this as fact and assuming no U-boats were in sight, Lieutenant Radford moved in close to supervise the rescue, sending out the LST-644, a tank-landing craft, to pick up survivors. Assuming the area was safe, the *Regina* had stopped its engines about 275 metres from the stricken cargo ship. Suddenly a massive explosion erupted, obliterating the HMCS *Regina,* and when the water, smoke, steam, and oil settled, the *Regina* was nowhere to be seen. The corvette had gone to the bottom in thirty seconds, leaving only floating debris, oil, dead bodies, and struggling survivors. Donald McIntosh, from Saskatoon, who managed to survive the *Regina* sinking, describes the moment of the explosion:

*I had one particularly good pal. He was an engine room artificer from Canmore, Alberta. And his name was Joe Hellis. And Joe was on duty when the ship was torpedoed and of course, he died. Everybody in the engine room and boiler room died, nobody made it out. But Joe was a particularly good friend of mine.*

*I felt a rumble, like an explosion or something in the water. I grabbed my life jacket I guess and I ran up onto the quarter deck. We looked back at the convoy and we could see one of the ships was sinking down from the front of the bow. We went back. I guess the intent was to take the survivors off the ship. And this was a 10,000-ton [US] liberty freighter. So we went back there and we were standing on the quarterdeck of our ship [...] the* Ezra Weston *[...]. And it was going down slowly by the bow. And there was a deck cargo of trucks, cars and everything and as the angle increased, the vehicles were rolling off into the, the water. It was quite a sight to see. So, in a few minutes, we saw a lifeboat coming from the* Ezra Weston *and it had the entire crew of the* Ezra Weston *on it. And they were rowing towards us. And we were standing still, waiting for them to come, and all of a sudden, this tremendous explosion. Unbelievable.*

*We were later told by these fellows sitting in their rowboat [...] debris flew in the air and by the time it came down about 30 seconds, there was no sign of our ship at all. It just blew up. I was just on the quarterdeck and I remember the explosion, a great white sheet, and that's all I remembered until I was in the water. So I must have been blown off the ship, I didn't go off myself. Way down in the water, I really thought this is it, but all of a sudden, I popped up to the surface and I very fortunately had my life jacket on, because I can't swim a stroke, never could.*

Jim Hawley also recalls the sinking:

*And I just come off duty and walked up to the bridge, chum of mine, George Dick, he was on the signal lamp on the bridge and I was just heading up to see George and wham-mo, we got her. Just all hell. All I remember is being in the water and looking up and see the forecastle of the ship, where she split right in half when we got hit. And the forecastle went up and I could see the forecastle. I was scared because I thought it was going to come over on us because we were in the water. Oh, it got torpedoed, it split right in half.*

*Boy, I was lucky, I was above deck. All the guys below deck were killed. Everybody that was below deck, all the engine room, boiler room. The only guy below deck that got off was the guy that was on the wheel and he got washed out. Everybody else got killed.*

*We were floating around in the oil, that was the hardest part, the water was covered with oil. I forget how long it was we were in the water before we got picked up. An American landing craft picked us up.* (The Historica Memory Project)

## HMCS *Alberni*
*Flower Class corvette, torpedoed and sunk, August 21, 1944*

THE TRAGIC FATE OF THE HMCS *ALBERNI* CERTAINLY exemplifies the fact that total war precludes guaranteed survival, on either side. For four long years, the *Alberni*, aside from time off for refit and repairs, was in the thick of action. The diminutive Flower Class corvette built in the Yarrow shipyards in Esquimalt, British Columbia, was one of the early orders of warships for the RCN. Arriving in Halifax via the Panama Canal, it was quickly pressed into service.

From 1941 to 1944, the *Alberni* served in the Mediterranean, North Africa, the English Channel, and on convoy routes ranging across the North Atlantic. In 1942 alone, it rescued 145 survivors from torpedoed cargo ships and was heavily involved in the fight for convoy SC-42 which was attacked by over 15 U-boats. The ship was indirectly involved in the sinking of at least two U-boats and was credited with the "probable kill" of a third. The *Alberni* is also credited with putting its Oerlikon and pom-pom guns to good use in shooting down a Junkers 88 which attacked the ship at an altitude of only a few metres. On one occasion it barely missed hitting a mine and on another suffered a depth charge explosion just off the starboard. Damage was minimal and the young crew members of the *Alberni* were definitely not beset by boredom. By June 1944, the *Alberni* was involved in Operation Neptune, supporting the D-Day landings. It remained in the English Channel area and in September 1944, was involved in convoy escort duty from England to the landing beachhead.

Fate caught up to the *Alberni* on August 21, 1944. At around noon, just southeast of the Isle of Wight, heading alone to relieve the HMCS *Drumheller* from submarine patrol, it came into the periscope sights of Hans Joachim Forster, commander of *U-480*. There was no ASDIC warning as an acoustic torpedo struck the port side just aft of the engine room. Within seconds the ship had settled and was sinking rapidly and, less than a minute later, the proud and competent *Alberni* dropped beneath the waves. As with many attacks of such severity, most men below decks were trapped and killed outright or had not nearly enough time to save themselves. Those on deck were thrown or washed over the sides, or, if able, jumped for their lives without time to don life jackets. Acting-Lieutenant-Commander Ian H. Bell had no time whatsoever to issue orders as within seconds he was washed overboard. The sinking was so quick that there was no time to launch lifeboats or even carley floats.

Although the depth charges did not go off, there was a series of smaller boiler explosions as the ship went down. With no rescue ships in sight, the men in the water could only thrash around, helping and encouraging each other when they could, but all knew that, unless rescued soon, they would soon perish in the frigid waters.

Then providence stepped in. Two motor torpedo boats, returning from a Normandy patrol, had seen an explosion, come over to investigate, and found the still-dazed survivors. By this time, they had been in the water for forty-five minutes, many already having given up the struggle. The MTBs were able to pick up thirty-one of the ship's company, but another fifty-nine crew members would not be coming home.

Murray T. "Curly" Copot survived the *Alberni* sinking and describes the moment the ship got hit and went down:

> *I guess I must have got hit in the head or something but all at once, I sort of woke up and it was kind of dark, underwater and I wasn't too sure whether I was going up or down. But all at once, it started to get brighter, so at that time, I said, well, I'm going the right way [...] so I popped up and when I saw the bow of the ship going down, I broke all records in the water to get away from getting sucked down again [...] and it was about that time that I said, my mother can't get a telegram because it would kill her. So there's something in prayers also.* (The Historica Memory Project)

### HMCS *Magog*
*River Class frigate, torpedoed, October 14, 1944*

THE *MAGOG*, COMMANDED BY LIEUTENANT LEWIS DENNIS Quick, had been commissioned less than six months prior to sinking, but served as escort for several convoys before it was attacked by *U-1223* in the Gulf of St. Lawrence off Pointe des Monts. The acoustic torpedo took twenty metres off the frigate's stern, killing three crew members and wounding three others. The ship, still afloat, was taken in tow by the HMCS *Toronto*, then the HMCS *Shawinigan*. Finally the severely damaged *Magog* was towed to Quebec City where the damage was assessed. Sadly, the *Magog* was beyond repair and was eventually sold as scrap. While the loss of life was not as high as it might have been had a direct hit been scored, the loss of three crew members was considered, to those who survived, as important as the loss of the HMCS *Shawinigan* a few weeks later on November 24, or the loss of any other Allied ship, for that matter.

Lost in the October attack on the *Magog* were: Petty Officer Thomas E. Davies, RCNVR; Ordinary Seaman Gordon T. Elliot, RCNVR; and Able Seaman Kenneth J. Kelly, RCNVR.

To those families living along the shores of the St. Lawrence River, watching U-boat attacks and subsequent chases was nothing new, but it still generated much excitement. The wife of the local lighthouse keeper, Alphonsia Fafard, described the *Magog* incident in colourful detail, stating, "The families of the Pointe, Fafards, and Comeaus alike, then witnessed a splendid maritime ballet; the frigates and corvettes, with all their alarms sounding, covered the convoy in a thick artificial fog, while geysers shot up here and there as depth charges were launched."

## HMCS *Skeena*
### Destroyer, lost in storm, October 24, 1944

IN 1928, CANADA'S FLEDGLING NAVY CONSISTED OF A mere handful of obsolete ships donated by the British Navy. But, determined to build a navy of its very own, in 1931 the Canadian government granted approval to have two ships built in British shipyards and modified to Canadian specifications.

These two Acasta "A" Class destroyers included a few new features, such as strengthened hulls to withstand heavy ice conditions, steam-heated crew quarters, and improved ventilation and refrigeration systems—enough extras and changes to make the British sailors truly envious.

Commissioned in June 1931, shortly after the completion of its sister ship the HMCS *Saguenay*, the *Skeena* served Canada well in peacetime for the next eight years. When the war began, both the *Skeena* and *Saguenay* served as escorts on the Atlantic crossings. The *Skeena* rescued survivors from at least four torpedoed merchant ships and took active part in the sinking of *U-588*. The ship also won battle honours for its work in the English Channel during D-Day operations.

On October 24, 1944, the *Skeena* was involved in anti-submarine patrols off Iceland when it encountered severe storm conditions, making it necessary to head for shelter in port at Reykjavik. The ship reached Videy Harbour safely, anchored, and settled in to wait out the storm. But as the weather worsened considerably during the night, the *Skeena*'s anchor could not hold, and before it was noticed, the ship had drifted away from its mooring and was driven broadside onto the rocks by the raging storm. Try as it might, the hapless destroyer could not break free and conditions were too dangerous for any ship to get close enough to help. Many men, believing that the ship would break up or roll over at any time, followed the captain's order to abandon ship and went to the carley floats. One of the three floats overturned, spelling disaster for those thrown into the frigid sea. The captain, now realizing that any further attempts to leave the ship would cost more lives, rescinded his order, praying the *Skeena* would survive the night in one piece. Luckily, by morning a line from shore attached to the ship and the remaining crew were able to be safely taken off.

There were fifteen crew members lost at the final count. Thirty-five more were sent to the local US military hospital suffering from severe hypothermia and shock. Although the *Skeena*'s record was exemplary, having served Canada for nearly fifteen years, it is perhaps unfair that the ship is remembered for its tragic end rather than its triumphs.

## HMCS *Shawinigan*
*Flower Class corvette,*
*torpedoed and sunk, November 24, 1944*

IN MOST CASES WHEN A TORPEDO STRATEGICALLY HITS A warship, there is a loss of life. Indeed, of the twenty-four RCN warships lost in the line of duty, three went down with no survivors. The HMCS *Shawinigan* was the third and last Canadian ship to suffer this terrible fate.

Another of the original Flower Class corvettes commissioned in September 1941, the *Shawinigan* usually worked the convoy routes in Canadian waters, although, for a short period, it was assigned to the St. John's–Londonderry run. The corvette, its crew consisting of a full complement of ninety-one men, was, aside from time outs for refits, repairs, and alterations, generally glad to go wherever it was needed in whatever capacity, be it convoy escort, anti-sub, or harbour patrols. Commanded originally by Acting-Lieutenant-Commander C. P. Balfry, the *Shawinigan* was also captained by Lieutenant R. S. Williams, Lieutenant W. E. Callan, and, at the time of her sinking, Lieutenant W. J. Jones.

On October 13, the SS *Caribou*, a large car and passenger ferry plying the Sydney–Port aux Basques route, was torpedoed and sunk with the loss of 137 lives. Only one ship had escorted the *Caribou* on its fatal final crossing.

Two other warships were now assigned to the new ferry, SS *Burgeo*. On November 24, 1944, the *Shawinigan* and the *Sassafras*, a US Coast Guard cutter, had just finished escorting the *Burgeo* into Port aux Basques, where it would depart late the next day for the return to Sydney. The *Shawinigan* would be the lone escort and in the meantime the corvette would conduct submarine patrols in the area until it was time to rendezvous with the SS *Burgeo* the following morning. The *Shawinigan* never showed up for the rendezvous and in fact was never seen again, along with eighty-five men of its crew of ninety-one. The captain of the *Burgeo* had maintained radio silence until he reached Sydney, which delayed the start of the search, by which time it was much too late to help survivors. After three days of searching, all that was found of the *Shawinigan* were six bodies, an oil slick, and a few empty carley floats. What must have been the final destruction of the HMCS *Shawinigan* was heard on land by several people, including Randal James, who claims he heard what sounded like a "case of dynamite followed by a rumble like thunder." Another man claimed he also heard "an explosion followed a few minutes later by a roar like thunder." Apparently even the master of the *Burgeo* said he heard a "loud noise" that night, and his wife said "the house began to tremble."

The disappearance of the *Shawinigan* remained a mystery until the end of the war, when interrogated prisoners of *U-1228* revealed the corvette's final moments. The captain of *U-1228*, Friederich-Wilhelm Marienfeld, was not having a good patrol. His new schnorkel was not working properly, thus limiting the ship's ability to manoeuvre and putting his crew at a dangerous disadvantage. On the calm night of November 24, Marienfeld was cruising the surface checking on his repairs, which he found to be insufficient for a prolonged patrol. No U-boat commander wanted to arrive back home with an empty "kill" sheet, but what else was to be done? Just as he ordered his boat to the proper heading for the journey home, the *Shawinigan* was sighted. Taking a few minutes to get into an ideal firing and getaway position should the torpedoes miss, Marienfeld ordered a Gnat T-5 electric homing torpedo unleashed at a range of 4,000 yards. The aim of the *U-1228* was true as, within four minutes, the *Shawinigan's* stern, as Marienfeld later described it, erupted in a "high, 50 metre, large explosion with a heavy shower of sparks, after collapse of explosion column, only 10 metres high now, then smoke cloud, destroyer disappeared." Marienfeld had in fact mistaken the corvette for a RN destroyer which sank fast with no indication of survivors. Marienfeld also claims he could still detect noises from what he assumed was another enemy ship, so he decided to make his escape.

## HMCS *Clayoquot*
*Minesweeper, torpedoed and sunk, December 24, 1944*

THE DIMINUTIVE MINESWEEPER *CLAYOQUOT*, ON ACTIVE DUTY since construction in Prince Rupert, British Columbia, in 1941, dutifully went where it was needed. Although built as a minesweeper, the ship was used more often than not in convoy escort operations, as the large number of mines expected to be sown by enemy subs did not materialize. Much of the *Clayoquot's* work was with the Gulf Escort Force, the Halifax Local Defence Force, and the Sydney Escort Force. At one point, it served as a training ship for air and sea warfare out of HMCS *Cornwallis*. By December 1944, the *Clayoquot* was back with the Halifax force. This suited the standard crew of seventy-seven seamen and six officers. Many of the men aboard were Maritimers, and shore leave was quite frequent.

With Christmas coming up, most aboard were undoubtedly looking forward to partaking in a bit of the holiday spirit. But until then, work had to be done. A few days earlier, on December 21, U-806 had sunk a US ship, the *Samtucky*. The *Clayoquot*, along with the frigate *Kirkland Lake* and another minesweeper, the *Transcona*, were detailed to sweep the area near convoy XB-139, which was just heading out. But U-806 was still out there, undetected as the *Clayoquot* sailed into its path. In fact, U-806 had thought it must have been picked up by the *Clayoquot*'s ASDIC, since the ship had turned sharply to attack. But the *Clayoquot* was simply manoeuvring to find its assigned position in the convoy. The commander of U-806, Klause Hornbostel, decided he and his rather inexperienced crew had best get out while they could, but not without a parting shot. Unleashing a T-5 homing torpedo at the fast-closing *Clayoquot*, Hornbostel dove quickly, lest his sub attract its own torpedo. A little over a minute later, a

*Survivors of the minesweeper* HMCS Clayoquot, *which was torpedoed by* U-806 *in December 1944. The* HMCS Fennel *took part in picking up survivors.* (Library and Archives Canada PA-136255)

thunderous explosion occurred as the torpedo slammed in to the stern section of the *Clayoquot*. Tom Burnside of Ontario was aboard the *Kirkland Lake* and describes the strike as he saw it: "I was on the quarterdeck, probably avoiding work, talking to Guy Gugeon, who had finally relieved me. I had just said 'Doesn't that sweeper look sharp in her new paint job,' when her stern blew to bits in a cloud of smoke and steam. Her survivors quickly took to the water and she sank stern first within minutes."

Ten minutes can be a blessing for a stricken ship, and all the practiced drills came into play as the men of the *Clayoquot* went about their survival procedures in a professional, almost calm manner. Luckily the *Transcona* and *Fennel* were there immediately to pick up the seventy-five survivors, all within forty minutes. Nonetheless, eight men were lost, having been killed outright by the explosion or trapped in their cabins as the ship went down. At least two of the trapped men were seen to be clawing at the porthole windows in terrified desperation as the ship sank below the waves. But alas, nothing could be done to save them.

In the case of the *Clayoquot*, a much greater tragedy was averted. But the men aboard these small warships knew they lived a precarious existence. The U-boat war was unpredictable at best: no place at sea was truly safe, and the enemy was silent and deadly.

### The Sinking of U-877

*Our ship was a Castle Class corvette. She was a little over a thousand tons. It was a modern corvette and we were more comfortable than the early ones. We were better armed, we had better ASDIC, better radar, ASDIC being now known as sonar. We carried Squid, which was a mortar firing forward.*

*It fired 300-pound bombs forward. It went off on contact but it also had depth settings on it directly from the radar sets. And it was the brand new weapon at the time, was very secret, and we were kind of proud of it, to have this special weapon.*

*In December [1944], after our Christmas celebration, we sailed from Newfoundland and when we were about two days out, yeah, it was the 27th of December, we ran across a submarine who had blundered into the convoy. As far as I know, it was heading towards North America with the view to broadcasting weather reports, probably for the Battle of the Bulge or that was the intent.*

*We had attacked many things before that, schools of fish, wrecks. We never knew, we got these ASDIC contacts but we had fired depth charges and Squid, all kinds of things and never got a submarine. So when this particular action stations was called, we were out in the middle of the Atlantic, we didn't know what it was but we were ready to go and it could be a submarine.*

*Well, it wasn't until it landed on the surface, my action station happened to be a twin Oerlikon high angle gun for anti-aircraft primarily and it fired a 20mm explosive shell. We were out of range but I can still visually see this submarine still on the surface, black, ugly. All submarines are ugly. And there it was, on the surface. And we were out of range but we turned and we were heading directly for it to ram her. Our main gun started to fire but they missed it and before we got there, it sank. And then there were all these people in the water and these little, they weren't even boats, they were sort of floats. And they were clinging to them and our captain stopped the ship and we pulled them aboard. As far as I know, there was never any question of not picking them up. The HMCS Sea Cliff came in and picked the rest of them up but to have sunk a submarine after all these years and times they cross miserably, and seeing nothing and doing nothing. Sure, you were protecting ships but you had never seen anything you're protecting it from, but having got a submarine, we were in heaven. And cheers would go up around the ship for days after, all of a sudden, a bunch of guys would cheer the fact we got a submarine, it was quite amazing.*

*And there were a lot of other submarines sunk but there were a lot of ships that never sank a submarine or had any action with a submarine. So we were very pleased to not only have sunk it but to have proof that we sank it [...] we had fifty guys basically to prove that we sank the submarine.*

*The whole crew got off the submarine, and between our ship and the* HMCS *Sea Cliff, we picked up the whole crew. There was nobody killed, there was one man slightly injured where he hit his head when he came out of the hatch. And I forget how many, there were about fifty-five I think in the total submarine crew and we had about thirty of them. We fed them the same as we were getting. They were onboard for New Years and we happened to have chicken and ice cream and so they got chicken and ice cream. We were going from Newfoundland to Britain, so we took them and we put them off on Gourock, Scotland, where they were taken ashore by a great guard of people with rifles and bayonets. And [when] we'd had them aboard, they'd become almost friendly. In fact, our first lieutenant and their first lieutenant became friends and were friends after the war.*

—*Gerald Wilkes, Able Seaman,* HMCS St. Thomas,
*courtesy* The Historica Memory Project

# 1945

DESPITE THE TIDE HAVING TURNED HEAVILY IN THE Allies' favour, 1944 and 1945 were the years of heaviest warship losses in the RCN. The German Navy had gotten a second wind with its implementation of the new schnorkel devices. In this period, eighteen RCN warships went down, including the terrible dockside fire at the Ostend docks in which five RCN motor torpedo boats were lost. U-boats were no longer a serious threat to Allied shipping, but were still deadly in lone encounters, especially near port entrances where warships could be singled out, targeted, and sunk. This was the case of the HMCS *Esquimalt*, which was torpedoed just outside Halifax Harbour a mere few weeks before the end of the war.

## RCN Motor Torpedo Boats (MTB)
### 459, 461, 462, 465, 456
*Lost in fire at Ostend, February 14, 1945*

BECAUSE OF THEIR SMALL SIZE AND LIMITED ARMAMENTS and range, the RCN flotillas of MTBs were never as well recognized as the much larger destroyers, corvettes, and frigates, but they are considered by many to be true unsung heroes among RCN warships of the Second World War. These small boats were designed as fast attack boats, effectively used in the English Channel, especially before, during, and after D-Day operations.

On the afternoon of February 14, 1945, the Canadian 29TH MTB Flotilla was safely berthed at Ostend, fitting and preparing for a scheduled patrol that night. Many of the crew were in their berths resting or asleep before the long night ahead. Minor service repairs, rearming, and refuelling were underway. The MTB 464 was in the process of draining water from one of its fuel tanks, but unknowingly pumped 190 litres of volatile fuel into the water. A great tragedy was about to occur.

It was never determined what ignited the high-octane fuel, but at about 1600 hours, the fuel in the water burst into flame. There was barely a chance to fight the fire as the flames quickly engulfed the MTBs. Ammunition and fuel tanks exploded, spreading the inferno to other ships. Windows throughout Ostend burst from the succeeding concussions, and death was everywhere. Many of the crews below decks never stood a chance as the fire raged. When it was all over, five of eight boats from the 29TH MTB Flotilla were lost as well as twenty-five crew members. The British Navy fared no better, as seven of its vessels were lost along with thirty-five men.

With the war nearing its conclusion it was decided to disband the 29TH Flotilla, despite an offer to join the RN's 65TH MTB Flotilla, and the remainder of the Canadian crew returned to Canada.

In recognition of the tragedy, and in commemoration of the men lost, a beautiful granite monument was erected near the area where the disaster occurred, with memorial services held on February 14 of each year.

### HMCS *Trentonian*
*Revised Flower Class corvette,
torpedoed and sunk, February 22, 1945*

BUILT AND LAUNCHED OUT OF THE KINGSTON SHIP-building Yards in 1943 as a corvette of the Increased Endurance Program, the *Trentonian*, with its complement of seven officers and ninety other ranks, served for nearly two years before falling victim, on February 22, to *U-1004*. The corvette was well-equipped with standard armaments and detection equipment. As well, the young but experienced crew was skippered by a well-liked and reliable commander, Lieutenant William Edward Harrison, RCNR, and later, at the time of sinking, Lieutenant Colin S. Glassco.

The *Trentonian* was involved in a friendly fire incident on June 12, 1944, while escorting the HMCS *Monarch* as it laid underwater cable in the English Channel. A series of miscommunication errors with an American destroyer, the USS *Plunkett,* resulted in the British and Canadian ships coming under friendly fire. The *Trentonian* was not hit but the HMCS *Monarch* was damaged, incurring severe injuries and loss of life among its crew. Fortunately the *Trentonian* was the only Canadian warship to come under friendly fire by an American warship during the Second World War.

The corvette continued to serve, with escort duty and anti-sub detection being among its primary duties. The crew of the *Trentonian* were aware of the dangers of a lurking U-boat ready to unleash havoc on an unsuspecting vessel. Still, complacency and, to a degree, boredom, often crept in and vigilance lessened, especially with the end of the war so near. ASDIC was still far from perfect, and a "hit" on an object often turned out to be unconfirmed and unreliable. The U-boats, on the other hand, were just as lethal as they had been from the war's onset.

In the early morning of February 22, 1944, the *Trentonian*, along with a British torpedo boat, was about eleven kilometres off the British coast escorting a small convoy of ten ships. Suddenly, with no warning, the SS *Alexander Kennedy*, one of the cargo ships, suffered a terrible explosion and began to go down. The *Trentonian* immediately went to action stations and began searching for the sub, quickly finding an

ASDIC contact. But it was too late. The *Trentonian* took a direct hit from a deadly Gnat torpedo. Flames and splintered steel erupted as the missile blew a hole in the corvette's starboard quarter.

Both ships sank in about fifteen minutes: enough time to allow the crew to abandon ship without severe losses. The *Trentonian*'s commander, Lieutenant Glassco, had ordered all crewmen to wear life jackets when on deck, and this unpopular decree undoubtedly saved a lot of lives. The British torpedo boat was there to pick up survivors, and as a result the men were no more than an hour in the freezing water. Despite these fortunate circumstances, six crew members were lost, but ninety-six were safely rescued. The *Alexander Kennedy* lost one man while eighteen were rescued from the merchant ship.

Over the years, the surviving crew members of HMCS *Trentonian* had several reunions and remembrances for their beloved ship. Many spoke fondly of the good times while serving under Commanders Harrison and Glassco, the latter who, in fact, only had a chance to captain the ship for twenty-three days. As Stoker First Class Bruce Kier recalls, "We would hear the stories from other ships and how their officers were and we were glad we were on *Trentonian*. Everyone got along." Kier also recalls how well the city of Trenton, after which the ship was named, supported them by sending food, knitting, and treats. "They also sent us a washing machine, a piano which no one knew how to play, a saxophone, drums," Kier remembers. "It gave us a great deal of satisfaction during those periods of boredom and at our later reunions we had the opportunity to say thank you."

## HMCS *Guysborough*

*Bangor Class minesweeper, torpedoed and sunk
in the English Channel, March 17, 1945*

THE INHERENT DANGERS OF NAVAL WARFARE ARE MANY, and each and every sailor aboard any warship is well aware that chaos could erupt at any given moment. In the case of the HMCS *Guysborough*, a hopeful escape from disaster was not to be, as the minesweeper suffered the indignity of first being lightly wounded, then receiving a *coup de grâce*, which ended in the tragic loss of the ship and fifty-one crew members.

Built in the North Vancouver Shipyards for the RN and launched in July 1941, the *Guysborough* was transferred to the RCN. Over the next several years, the Bangor Class minesweeper served on escort forces on both sides of the Atlantic, with duties ranging from minesweeping and sub detection, to rescue work. On March 10, 1944, the *Guysborough* picked up a crew of twenty men in a lifeboat from a US ship that had been abandoned after striking a drifting log in a raging sea, which severely damaged the ship's steering gear.

On March 17, 1945, at 1850 hours, U-868 was cruising an area near the Azores when it spotted the *Guysborough* sailing alone. The RCN minesweeper had just completed a fuelling stop and was heading back to rejoin its convoy when U-868 fired an acoustic Gnat torpedo, designed to impact the ship's stern, drawn by the sound of its propellers. Though the *Guysborough* was towing CAT gear (Canadian Anti-Acoustic Torpedo—a noisemaker towed behind the ship to deflect incoming enemy torpedoes), the torpedo still struck home. It was later assumed that the CAT was towed too close to the ship to confuse the torpedo. Although the blast caused severe damage and a list to port, the work done by damage control crews was able to stop water from coming in. But the ship was now dead in the water. If the sub had left the area, everything would be all right until help arrived. Unfortunately, this was not to be. At 1935 hours, forty-five minutes after the initial hit, U-868 fired a *coup de grâce*, hitting the minesweeper starboard amidships. There was still hope as the men abandoned ship. Up to now there was only two men killed from the explosions. The ship's larger motor boat and smaller whaler were too damaged to be used, so the five carley boats were filled, one overloaded.

Hope for a quick rescue faded as the hours passed. The crew passed the time singing and praying over the next nineteen hours, but the men were weakening fast in the frigid weather. On the overcrowded raft, thirty-six died of hypothermia and another thirteen succumbed to the elements, among those who died on the other five rafts. By the time the HMS *Inglis* showed up, ending the nightmare, fifty-one men had died with forty survivors.

As in other such cases, heroes came forward. In one case Jack Cox from Ontario had been playing checkers when the torpedo hit. Later, in a carley float, weak and fading, Jack turned to his friend Ralph Kaple, from Sault Ste. Marie, saying, "Ralph, tell the wife it was my move." Then he simply dove off the carley float and he was gone, giving room in the overcrowded float to his shipmates. Such acts of heroism were not uncommon.

### Surviving the HMCS Saguenay

*The HMCS Saguenay was torpedoed 200 miles off the coast of Ireland, and nineteen killed and twenty-one injured. I was a radio operator, and I was in the remote control office, and not too far away from where the torpedo struck, about eighty feet, I think.*

*I had the door of the office ajar about four inches for venti-
lation. And when the torpedo struck, there was blue flame
oscillating back and forth. It just filled the whole entire
doorway. Also the smell of cordite. And later there were
other smells from the fire.*

*Got permission to close down the watch I was on, and I went
out on the upper deck to check the antennas. And I looked up
and the mast was broken. And the antennas were just dangling
about. So I went and reported that to the head telegrapher, and
he was trying to send out a distress message. When I told him
this, he said, well, we'd better switch on another transmitter,
which he did and the only other one we had was a spark [gap]
transmitter, which was something I guess they had gotten during the First World War. It was a shaky proposition. We didn't
know if that message would get out or not.*

*We were lucky that the message did get out [...] the fire
was getting bad, so the captain gave the order to us to standby
to abandon ship. And we put down the guardrails and, of
course, [we had] the carley float, which was my abandon ship
station, halfway over the side and sat on the inboard side; and
I and a chum of mine were sitting there; and [I] took his hand,
and said, well, I hope you make it. And he says, there's not a
chance that we'll make it (this was in December); this water
is so cold that we wouldn't last five minutes—it'll be an easy
death. That was a very comforting thought.*

*About dawn, HMS Highlander, a British destroyer,
appeared on the scene. And there was a great shout of joy
from the entire ship. Apparently our distress message had
gotten through.*

*Later on, I was in the hospital, [Royal Naval] Stonehouse
Military Hospital in Plymouth, and the chap in the next bed
to me had been on an oil tanker that got blown up. He had his
eyelids grafted; he had a broken pelvis, broken legs, broken*

*arms. It was hard to imagine why he had stayed alive. As I say, they grafted, he had been blown into the water and there was oil in the water and the oil was on fire. It had burned his eyelids off; and he had grafted eyelids.*

*He used to cheer me up when I got depressed. He was a Newfoundlander. He was a religious person. I can't remember. And he always, always had a positive outlook; and I just couldn't understand him. All he could do. At that time, I was very depressed as a result of the killings of my shipmates. It had very great mental effect on me. At that time, they didn't have any facilities that they have today for shellshock, or whatever they want to call it. And so I suspect that's why it still bothers me. I don't think it will ever leave me.*

*—Arlo M. Moen, Nova Scotia,*
*courtesy* The Historica Memory Project

## HMCS *Esquimalt*
*Bangor Class minesweeper,*
*torpedoed and sunk, April 16, 1945*

THE *ESQUIMALT* WAS A MINESWEEPER OF THE BANGOR CLASS and has the distinction of being the last Canadian warship sunk in the Second World War. Many felt this was a disaster which should not have occurred, at least not to the extent of forty-four crewmen being lost. The total affair was a tragedy of errors, omissions, unpreparedness, and complacency and sadly, the drama unfolded practically within view of the lights of Halifax.

The *Esquimalt* was, by 1945, a veteran of offshore harbour patrols and by April 1945 was involved in regular anti-sub sweeps in the Halifax Harbour approaches. U-boat activity was suspected in the area during the previous two weeks, but not confirmed. On April 16, the *Esquimalt* was on its regular run on a calm, clear night and was expected to rendezvous with the HMCS *Sarnia*. These operations were routine, and, knowing the war would end soon, many of the crewmen's thoughts may well have been on other matters. At around 0400 hours, the *Esquimalt* made what was thought to be submarine contact, so depth charge action stations were sounded. A sweep was made of the area, but nothing was found. At 0610 hours, the depth charge crews were ordered to stand down. The radar, obsolete as it was, was not being used, nor was the CAT gear. As well, the *Esquimalt* was not zigzagging, a serious breach of naval regulations.

But there was indeed a sub out there, waiting in the shallow, rocky bottom just five kilometres from shore, knowing ASDIC, especially a primitive one such as that the *Esquimalt* carried, would have problems distinguishing a large rock from a submarine's hull. U-190 picked up the pinging of a minesweeper's hull, and waited. No attack came, so the sub, under Leutnant Hans-Edwin Reith, ventured to the surface to take a look. Reith quickly spotted the *Esquimalt* at about 1,500 metres away. A few moments later, the minesweeper suddenly turned and made directly for U-190. Thinking he was under attack, Lieutenant Reith, at around 0630 hours, quickly released a Gnat torpedo from his stern tube. Joe Wilson, the ASDIC operator, had been listening intently, but detected no echo that could be reported as a U-boat hull. He did, however, hear the torpedo strike the starboard quarter. Power was cut instantly, leaving the ship in darkness. The *Esquimalt* began to tilt and list immediately. There was no time for a flare, radio message, flag, or any kind of signal. The larger lifeboats could not be released as the men scrambled for the carley floats.

Sadly, twenty-eight on board the ship were killed outright by the explosion or, trapped by wreckage, could not make it out in the four minutes it took the ship to go down. Still, forty-three men were able to make it to carley floats, hopeful that they would be picked up in short order.

The signal station in Halifax tried to contact the *Esquimalt* at 1041 hours but got no response. This should have raised alarms, but the station failed to inform the watch officer. Also, alarms should have been raised when the *Esquimalt* failed to rendezvous with the *Sarnia*. In fact, it was not until 1130 hours that morning that shore command became worried and finally took action. Meanwhile, the men aboard the carley floats, many dressed in light clothing, were angry, frustrated, and scared. At one point an airplane flew overhead, but mistook the floats as small fishing vessels. At another point, two boats came within three kilometres from the men, but did not see them or hear their cries for help. It was only by 1230 hours that the survivors were finally spotted and picked up.

Of the forty-three men who escaped into the carley floats, sixteen succumbed to exposure in the six hours in the open sea. An inquest, considered unsatisfactory by many, was subsequently held, but no direct blame was attached to any one person. It was felt that, because the war was now over, there would be no purpose in censuring anyone.

*U-190* got clean away, hiding for a week in shallow, rocky waters. With the cessation of fighting, *U-190* gave itself over to the victors.

### We Were Young Then

*The 31st of August I picked up a ship, 1944, the old HMCS Acadia [a hydrographic survey ship commissioned into the Royal Canadian Navy as a training vessel]. That was, for me, it was very interesting. I was part of the regular crew and I was just as young as a lot of the new entries. We were on training. We were tied up with HMCS Cornwallis [Royal*

Canadian Navy training base in Deep Brook, Nova Scotia]
and we used to take draftees out on training, ten days, two
weeks at a time.

Everything from maintenance to scrubbing decks, to
lowering life rafts, to turns at the helm, on watch, at night
and daytime, whatever [...] gunnery practices, general
seamanship.

The navy was different. There was a danger all the time,
but I don't know. You had your crew that you depended on,
all your shipmates. You're all young and aggressive, and it
was exciting, very exciting.

I would have liked to have picked up, when I was drafted
aboard ship, I would have liked to have picked up a newer,
more modern ship and got over there. But you know, you
don't have a choice, you go where they tell you. That's, you
know, some of the fellows I enlisted with ended up in the
Pacific, but by the time they got there, it was pretty well over
because that was late 1944. So you go wherever they send
you, you go, that's it.

There's always a lot of laughs and a lot of friendship. You
make a lot of friends when you're onboard ship. You're all
brothers in arms is what you are.

You know, I don't think Canadians realize how close
Eastern Canada was, how they were involved in the war
effort. The Germans' U-190 sank the Esquimalt minesweeper, right over the Halifax Harbour, three weeks before
the war ended [Esquimalt was lost on April 16, 1945; the
war with Germany ended on May 8, 1945]. And we were
in Halifax at that time. That was an eye opener, you know.
They were there. And I had spent about six weeks up, before I
picked up the ship, up in Sydney, Nova Scotia. They had a flotilla of motor torpedo boats there; and every evening, they
would leave and go out up into the St. Lawrence and cruise

*at night, looking for subs. And then they'd come in in the morning; and we would, I wasn't involved onboard the ships, but we had to close everything down and clean everything up and get ready for the next night, fuel them up; and that was part of my training at that time. It was close. The St. Lawrence, there were a lot of ships in 1944. I can't remember how many ships were lost, mostly freighters. But the war was right here.*

*When they sunk the* Esquimalt *there right outside of Halifax Harbour, it was thirty-nine that perished [forty-four of* Esquimalt's *seventy crew members were lost]. The* U-190 *sunk her just after daybreak and she didn't get an* SOS *out. They perished. The cold water, they got wet and cold and thirty-nine men off of that ship. That was very sad, when you figure the war was just about over.*

—Norman Young, Bathurst, New Brunswick,
*courtesy* The Historica Memory Project

## The Esquimalt *goes down—a German viewpoint*

*Every German submarine had four commissioned officers: the commanding officer, two watch officers and the chief engineer. The chief engineer was usually the highest seniority after the commanding officer, so if the commanding officer was incapacitated, the chief engineer would take over.*

*I was at that time, of course, not even twenty and having this responsible job; and I was responsible for the life of over fifty people, was really very, very satisfying. I was then transferred again as chief engineer to a large ocean-going submarine stationed in Lorient in France. And that was the* U-190.

*We got a new device installed on the submarine, the so-called schnorkel, a mast of the length of the periscope which*

*Survivors of the* RCN *minesweeper* HMCS Esquimalt *being rescued on April 16, 1945. Forty-four died in the sinking, which occurred a mere two weeks before Germany's surrender, and within sight of Halifax Harbour.* (Library and Archives Canada PA-157029)

*allowed us to suck air in while being submerged and enabling to run our diesel engines to charge the batteries without having to surface and expose ourselves to enemy aircraft. So that schnorkel was really the device which enabled us to survive during the last half of the year and the beginning of 1945.*

*We were ready to go out again in February 1945 and embarked on the last mission, which took us to Halifax, where we operated for something like fifty days under water, looking for cargo ships, to sink them, but which weren't there anymore—they had been transferred to other ports. So we were really idling around there outside Halifax all this time. Then came the day when we had a feeling, being under water, we were being picked up by* ASDICS, *the echo sounding device the Allies used to find submerged submarines, and which could be heard inside the submarine. So we had the feeling we had been picked up and found by a warship. We came up to the surface and saw a small warship approaching us at high speed. At which time, we sort of simply, in a mode of defence, shot one torpedo, an acoustic torpedo, which hit that warship and sank it. And that was the* HMCS Esquimalt, *the last Canadian warship sunk during the war.*

*This was routine. There was nothing very special about it. This is what we have been trained to do, and so one step followed the next one; and in the end, after we knew the* Esquimalt *was gone, we felt relatively safer then; and we were happy that we were still alive. This was sort of the, the tragedy of it. We assumed they had found us, but in actuality, they did not.*

*We went as far inshore as we could and put ourselves at the bottom to switch off all our equipment, not to make any noise and simply wait out what may happen. And being fully aware that being that close in shore, the [Royal] Canadian Navy had some many difficulties in finding us for the simple reason that the bottom of the ocean, at that place, is so covered with all kinds of metallic debris that the* ASDIC *operators in Canadian warships had a heck of a time in sorting out what echo might be a submarine and what echo might simply be a lost anchor or tin cans, or whatever. So we felt quite safe there, that nobody would find us, and we were quite justified in that assumption because nobody did and, a few days later, we went back on normal operations.*

*At the end of April, we ran out of food and fuel; and we had to stop our return to Germany to make it. That was the end of April. So we turned east, we left the Halifax area and about 300 miles southeast of Newfoundland, we received the order by radio from the German high command to surface, to tell the world in open language who we were and where we were, throw our ammunition overboard and wait for things to happen. In other words, for us, the war was over at that time.*

*The following night, we were picked up by two Canadian warships, HMCS Thorlock and HMCS Victoriaville, who intercepted us and took all the crew off our submarine except for myself, the chief engineer, and ten people to keep the boat running. In exchange, we had about thirty Canadian sailors on our submarine and we spent the next three days travelling to Bay Bulls, that's south of St. John's in Newfoundland. We arrived I think on the fourteenth of May.*

—*Oberleutnant Werner Hirchmann, Dusseldorf, Germany,*
*courtesy* The Historica Memory Project

By the end of the war, German recruitment was becoming very difficult. The once-high standards of recruitment and training demanded of Doenitz's men now dropped to inferior levels. A new type of sub was produced as a last-ditch effort to defend against the Allied onslaught. Called the Type XXI, it had greater speed and better propulsion and endurance. But most importantly, these new models were coated with a rubber substance which was supposedly able to absorb ASDIC. Initially promised for use in November 1944, the first of these new subs was finally launched a week before the German surrender.

In the end the RCN had sunk a total of 27 U-boats and 42 enemy surface ships, while losing 24 ships, including those by accident, in five theatres. Lost also were 1,797 seamen. Over 180 million tons of supplies were shipped successfully overseas as well as thousands of troops. By war's end the RCN had become the third-largest navy in the world, controlled the northwest sector of the Atlantic Ocean, and continued

*The German submarine* U-190 *was responsible for the sinking of the* RCN *minesweeper* HMCS Esquimalt *on April 16, 1945. The crew surrendered to* RCN *authorities on May 11, 1945, following the end of hostilities.* (Library and Archives Canada PA-145584)

to build on its anti-sub capabilities in the postwar years. Perhaps never enough credit can be given to the men aboard these Canadian ships, both military and cargo, for against the U-boats they faced a formidable foe, often amidst the terrible weather conditions of the North Atlantic Ocean.

# CHAPTER THREE

# MERCHANT SHIPS LOST IN THE ST. LAWRENCE

MUCH CAN AND HAS BEEN SAID ABOUT THE RESOLUTE performance of the stalwart fleet of RCN warships, and rightly so, but neither should the brave crews of the merchant ships ever be forgotten. The Canadian Merchant Navy was created in 1939 and had about 38 ocean-going merchant vessels. By war's end, 410 cargo vessels had been built in Canada, carrying everything including clothing, foodstuffs, fuel, steel, lumber, jeeps, tanks, aircraft, munitions, and guns. Many of the crews were volunteers and had received training at special schools. Merchant ships were not heavily armed, but in most cases had small guns to fend off light attacks. These men had no ranks or uniforms, and were paid little.

The plight of the merchant seamen improved greatly as more escort ships were turned out. In fact almost 90 percent of the casualties suffered by Canadian merchant seamen occurred before the end of 1942. Lost were seventy-five cargo vessels that strove so diligently to arrive at their destination unharmed, many protected by a convoy escort of only two ships. It is imperative that these men be honoured for their vital and ceaseless war effort.

## ss *Nicoya* and ss *Leto*
*Torpedoed and sunk, May 11–12, 1942*

DURING THE FIRST FEW MONTHS OF 1939, U-BOAT attacks occurred mainly in the waters surrounding Britain, including the English Channel. With the fall of France and Norway, new bases were used and as more U-boats became available and successes mounted, the German attacks spread further across the Atlantic where a fertile and less protected hunting ground was to be found along Canadian coastlines. By 1942, hundreds of Allied merchant ships had already been lost as the war at sea moved considerably closer to home. During these years, Canadian coastal defences had been shored up somewhat by posting lookout stations along the Gaspé and St. Lawrence shorelines. Heavy guns were placed in various strategic locations while thousands of volunteers came forward to help man these defences.

Although warned by Canadian Prime Minister Mackenzie King that enemy attacks were a real possibility, the people of Gaspé were thoroughly shocked when, on the night of May 11, 1942, a loud explosion thundered inland from twenty-four kilometres out to sea. One Gaspésien likened it to an earthquake. A torpedo, fired from U-553, under the command of Kapitänleutnant Karl Thurmann and in territory with only light air cover, struck the merchant carrier *Nicoya*, ripping open the port side so badly that it sunk in virtually seconds. Crew members scrambled for their lives, trying to reach the lifeboats, or anything buoyant, until help arrived. As Captain

E. H. Brice stated later, "There was so much steam, oil, noise, and fire that it was impossible to give orders, even to see."

Seventy of the seventy-six crew members were safely rescued, but six others were lost. For Kapitänleutnant Thurmann, that May night was not yet over. An hour after sinking the unescorted *Nicoya*, U-553 got the also-unescorted SS *Leto* in its periscope sights. Using a single torpedo, Thurmann struck the engine room of the *Leto*, which went down so quickly that only a single lifeboat and one raft were able to be used. The men had to swim for their lives.

Of the forty-three listed crew, thirty-one survived. Several of the crew who perished were trapped in the engine room and suffered the fate of drowning or being scalded to death by the steam.

Alerted by debris being washed up on the Gaspé shore, fishermen from the tiny villages of L'Anse-à-Valleau and Chloridorme helped pick up survivors, bringing them to their own homes and giving them such care that they needed no hospitalization. Several area residents had suspected something was amiss that evening when one man, local lighthouse keeper Joseph Ferguson at Cap-des-Rosiers, claimed he had seen a strange "stovepipe" sticking out of the water. As well, other villagers noticed large holes punched through fishing nets and a v-shaped turbulence in the water which they claimed resembled a periscope's wake. Though this was reported to the authorities, nothing was done.

The war had indeed reached the shores of Canada, albeit in an accidental sort of way as Kapitänleutnant Thurmann, seeking calmer water to affect engine repairs, wasn't planning any attack unless the opportunity presented itself, which it clearly did. Noting well that the convoy runs from Quebec and Montreal were weakly protected, Thurmann realized he was indeed in fertile hunting grounds. In fact, a single

Bangor Class minesweeper, a couple of motor launches, and two yachts armed with barely more than a machine gun were protecting the whole area. Although warships were being produced quickly, there just wasn't yet enough to go around. As a result, and despite the addition of five Flower Class corvettes in the St. Lawrence area, Canadian merchant and warships would continue to be targets of German U-boats.

After the *Nicoya* and *Leto* sinkings, Ottawa ordered a blackout on further enemy encounters in Canadian waters, however, rumours of a German landing, or even an invasion, soon abounded as more losses were made apparent. These initial attacks were the first time Canada had been attacked on its own territory since the War of 1812 and they gave the country an impetus to further challenge and growing U-boat threat.

### *Friendship*

*Yeah, I wanted to join the army but I was turned down. I tried the Merchant Navy. The Merchant Navy then [in 1941], we were short of men; like ships, they were short of ships too. So I joined the Merchant Navy.*

*You had to watch for everything, for leaks and had to watch for submarines. If you were lucky enough, you got clear of them. And the Germans, they were well-posted and well-trained. They could hit that torpedo anywhere they want.*

*At the end of the day, you went to bed; you didn't know where you were going to be the next morning. It was always that on your mind, what to do. Your best friend was a life preserver. That was your best friend, because you'd never know when you had to use it. There were two bunks in a row; you always had it with you. I used to like hearing the water hitting the bow of the ship; it would put you to sleep, it was like music. Some had it so hard, some so easy. A number were crippled. I myself, I was lucky, never got torpedoed. But I used to think about it often, going to bed at night, where I'd be in the morning. You'd never know that. It was so nice to see the sun.*

—Leslie Kenneth Main, New Carlisle,
*courtesy* The Historica Memory Project

## ss *Dinaric,* ss *Hainault,* ss *Anastassios Pateras*
### *Torpedoed, July 6, 1942*

THE CONVOY QS-15, INCLUDING THE MERCHANT SHIPS
ss *Dinaric,* ss *Hainault,* and ss *Anastassios Pateras,* was travelling on its way from Rimouski to Sydney, then on to the UK, on July 6, 1942. Just off Cap-Chat, however, U-132, under Kapitänleutnant Ernst Vogelsang, was on the prowl. At about 0520 hours, Vogelsang targeted the convoy and made his move on the merchant ships. He fired three torpedoes hoping for a triple-kill, and managed to hit two ships. The ss *Hainault,* a 4,300-ton Belgian merchant steamer, was heading for Sydney with a deck cargo of trucks. When it was hit, only one man was killed and two injured out of the full crew of forty-five aboard. Struck by another torpedo from U-132 was the Greek steamer ss *Anastassios Pateras,* which lost three of twenty-nine crew members.

Less than an hour later, Vogelsang would get his triple-kill when he caught up with the ss *Dinaric,* part of that same convoy. The *Dinaric* was hit in the engine room by a single torpedo, the explosion killing four sailors. Fortunately, the ship foundered but did not sink, allowing the remaining thirty-four crew members to be rescued safely. The *Dinaric* was taken in tow but foundered on July 9, before it could be salvaged.

## ss *Frederika Lensen*
*Torpedoed by U-132, July 20, 1942*

VOGELSANG AND HIS CREW ABOARD U-132 WERE NOT YET finished with the Gulf of St. Lawrence. On July 20, in broad daylight, Vogelsang, near Anticosti Island, brought his sub to the surface and was actually inside the convoy QS-19, sailing undetected. Like a fox in a chicken coop, Vogelsang took his time and picked out a likely target. The ship was the SS *Frederika Lensen*, an aging 4,367-ton steam merchant ship sailing in ballast. Vogelsang fired a single torpedo that hit the steamer amidship, devastating the engine room and bursting its boiler. Four men were killed instantly. They were Robert James Spence, Abudul Rajack, Ali Edris, and Ali Mossadden. Several escort ships in the convoy immediately turned and went after the U-boat, including a corvette and a fairmile. *U-132* dove to 160 metres, remained still, and hoped for the best. Eventually the attack ships exhausted the depth charge supply and went off to pick up the *Lensen's* 42 survivors. The *Lensen*, despite being severely damaged, was able to be towed and beached, a complete loss, and its back broken.

## ss *Chatham*
*Torpedoed, August 27, 1942*

THIS 5,649-TON AMERICAN-OWNED CARGO STEAMER was working for Goose Bay and Bluie, out of Sydney, Nova Scotia, when it was attacked and sunk in the Strait of Belle Isle. Besides being loaded with 150 tons of food supplies, the *Chatham* was also carrying a crew and 428 passengers.

A lucrative target indeed for Kapitänleutnant Paul Hartwig, commander of *U-517*. After this first kill, Hartwig went on to sink 8 merchant vessels and a 900-ton RCN warship over a twenty-day period, and all within Canadian coastal waters of the Gulf of St. Lawrence.

At 1348 hours, a single torpedo struck the *Chatham*. The explosion did a tremendous amount of damage. The boilers, generators, and steering gear were destroyed as well as most of the lifeboats on the starboard side. The blast destroyed five decks, although luckily the steamer did not go down immediately, allowing several hundred passengers to man the remaining life boats and row successfully to shore. But another group of survivors in lifeboats decided to wait for rescue. They were to wait six long hours in the bitter cold until finally the *Mojave* arrived. Seven crewmen as well as seven passengers died in the disaster and Commander Hartwig, sensing easy targets, was not about to leave the area just yet.

## ss *Arlyn*
*Torpedoed and sunk, August 28, 1942*

THE ARLYN WAS A SMALL US-OWNED CARGO STEAMER WHICH, on August 28, 1942, found itself within the small convoy SG-6, just off Bell Island, Newfoundland. Unbeknownst to the convoy, *U-165* was on its trail. At about 2130 hours, Kapitan Eberhard Hoffmann fired a spread of four torpedoes, hoping for multiple hits. Two ships were hit: the SS *Arlyn* was wounded quite severely and the USS *Laramie* was damaged but lived to fight another day. Nine crew members and three officers from the *Arlyn* were lost in the attack. The *Arlyn* remained afloat but awash for another six hours before Paul Hartwig ordered a *coup de grâce* and fired a torpedo to finish the little steamer off.

## ss *Donald Stewart*

*Torpedoed and sunk, September 3, 1942*

ON SEPTEMBER 3, 1942, AT 0130 HOURS, U-517, UNDER command of one of the most successful German sub commanders, Kapitänleutnant Paul Hartwig, spotted the Canadian bulk carrier SS *Donald Stewart* heavily laden with cement and aviation fuel. The much-needed cargo was destined for the US Air Force Base under construction at Goose Bay, Newfoundland. A single torpedo was unleashed, striking the *Donald Stewart* near the engine room, a fatal blow which soon turned the ship and water surface into a mass of debris and flaming oil. Three crew members were killed.

The corvette HMCS *Weyburn* spotted U-517 and went at it with everything at its disposal. Firing its 4-inch guns, dropping depth charges, and even attempting to ram the sub was to no avail as the U-boat got away cleanly, leaving only death, destruction, and a great deal of frustration. The *Weyburn's* ASDIC system was in great part to blame, as it was not giving accurate and complete signals. This was due, it was suspected, to the varying gradients of warm and cooler water, as well as salinity content, conditions which were to hinder ASDIC performance in the Gulf of St. Lawrence throughout the war.

As a result of the attack, the new runway at Goose Bay was delayed for months. U-517 was also spotted by a RCAF Digby aircraft, which quickly dove in an attempt to hit the sub with depth charges. However, the explosives went off too soon, almost causing the airplane itself to crash. Additional bombers were called in from bases in Nova Scotia and Prince Edward Island, but the weather would just not cooperate, and a large fog bank settled over the Gaspé area, reducing visibility to nil. Consequently, the QS-33 convoy suffered the most of all flotillas during the Gulf contest. What was really galling to those involved in Canada's naval defence efforts in the Gulf were the reports put out by German radio, which extolled the U-boats' successes and called the RCN a "third-rate" navy.

## SS *Aeas*, SS *Mount Pindus*, SS *Mount Taygetus*, and SS *Oakton*

*Torpedoed and sunk, September 7, 1942*

BRITISH BUILT AND GREEK OWNED, THE 4,729-TON freighter *Aeas* was part of the ill-fated convoy QS-33 which was decimated by the German subs U-165 and U-518, under the commands of Eberhard Hoffmann and Paul Hartwig. Within twenty-four hours, these commanders sunk five Allied ships, including the armed RCN yacht HMCS *Raccoon*. Loaded with lumber and steel, the *Aeas* was found and targeted by U-165 just off Rimouski, Quebec, on the dark and overcast night of September 6. Easily dispatched by the German sub with a loss of two of the freighter's forty-one men, the convoy escort *Raccoon* quickly took up the chase but came under Kapitan Eberhard's sights and was soon dispatched. The skippers of U-165 and U-517 were working and communicating in tandem and knew the exact position of the now unescorted convoy QS-33, and the night was still young.

The woes of convoy QS-33 continued into September 7, thanks to the efforts of Paul Hartwig and U-517. Looking for a big score, at approximately 2300 hours, Hartwig fired a spread of torpedoes at QS-33. Three ships were hit, the SS *Mount Pindus*, SS *Mount Taygetus,* and SS *Oakton*. The 7,560-ton *Pindus*, which was carrying a valuable payload of 89 tanks, went down losing 2 from the crew of 37. The Greek steamer

*Mount Taygetus* soon followed the ss *Mount Pindus* to a watery grave as a result of U-517's devastating attack on the convoy QS-33, losing 2 men from the total crew of 28. In fact, the ss *Mount Pindus*, ss *Mount Taygetus*, and ss *Oakton* were all sunk within a minute of each other as the remainder of QS-33 plunged even further into complete disarray.

Second Cook Ted Read was literally thrown out of his bunk when several torpedoes struck his coal-carrying ship, the ss *Oakton*, on September 7, 1942. He certainly felt lucky to be alive as he watched his ship break in two and sink in three minutes within sight of Anticosti Island, Quebec. The fact that only three perished out of the *Oakton*'s crew of twenty was attributed to the captain's insistence of consistent emergency drills. The ss *Oakton* was one of three ships sunk that day by the notorious U-517 under command of Paul Hartwig. U-517 was sunk two days into its second patrol. Hartwig would spend the remainder of the war in an Allied prison camp.

## ss *Saturnus*, ss *Inger Elizabeth*
*Torpedoed and sunk, September 15, 1942*

IN THE MEANTIME, BEFORE HIS UNSUCCESSFUL SECOND mission, Hartwig continued to wreak havoc on Allied ships. On September 15, four days after destroying the RCN corvette HMCS *Charlottetown*, Hartwig teamed up once again with Eberhard Hoffmann as they zeroed in on the fifteen-ship convoy SQ-36. In fact, U-517 had been tracking the convoy for the past twenty-four hours, waiting until the time was right to attack. At 1833 hours, six kilometres from Cap des Rosiers, four torpedoes were fired at the convoy, one striking the ss *Saturnus* and one other hitting the ss *Inger Elizabeth*. Both ships went down within six minutes of each other. The

*Saturnus* took a hit in the stern which killed the gunner on the stern gun watch. The rest of the crew of thirty-six survived the blast and were able to abandon ship and row successfully to shore.

Three crew members were killed as a result of the torpedo attack on the *Inger Elizabeth*. The 2,160-ton Norwegian coal carrying steamer took the hit amidships near the engine room, and two men, 3$^{rd}$ Engineer Henrik Knag and Irish Trimmer Edward Mangan, were killed instantly. Able Seaman Brune, on lookout watch, jumped overboard when the explosion occurred. Unfortunately Brune could not swim and was never seen again. As the survivors were awaiting rescue in the lifeboats they watched for nearly ten minutes as a periscope slowly passed across the convoy and among the survivors huddled miserably in their lifeboats and carley floats, not unlike a shark leisurely studying its prey. This latest attack by U-517 would be Paul Hartwig's last successful sinking in the Gulf of St Lawrence. His final four attempts missed a convoy near Bell Island, and Hartwig headed for home. Nevertheless, his patrol resulted in the loss of 286 people and 31,000 tons of Allied ships. However, U-165 and Hoffmann were still hunting, as were other subs that quickly moved into the area when Hartwig left.

## ss *Joannis*
*Torpedoed and sunk, September 16, 1942*

THE SS *JOANNIS*, A GREEK CARGO STEAMER WEIGHING 3,667 tons, was travelling in convoy SQ-36 on September 16, 1942, heading down the mighty St. Lawrence. Paul Hartwig had advised fellow U-boat commander Hoffmann where to expect to find the convoy, and by 1010 hours, Hoffmann had the ss *Joannis* in his sights just a few kilometres northwest of Cap Chat. The *Joannis* took a fatal hit and went down in ten minutes but, luckily, with no fatalities. Three ships were targeted in the attack, however the other two, the ss *Essex Lance* and the American freighter *Pan York*, both survived to fight another day. Although U-165 was spotted and attacked the next day by a Hudson bomber out of Chatham, New Brunswick, Commander Hoffmann managed to escape and leave the area.

## ss *Carolus*
### *Torpedoed and sunk, October 9, 1942*

THE SS *CAROLUS* WAS STEAMING FROM GOOSE BAY TO Montreal, carrying a load of barrels as part of a small convoy of only seven ships. While convoys of this size usually travelled slowly with fewer escorts, making them more vulnerable to attack, this case was unusual because there were three corvette escorts. The *Carolus* was leading the six other ships and was deep into Canadian waters near Sainte-Flavie, Quebec, when targeted by U-69, under command of Ulrich Graf. The 2,245-ton former Danish steamer was hit by a torpedo and sunk to the bottom, taking eleven men. Cargo ships were much larger in tonnage than escort ships and tended to sink more slowly, giving crews much more time to abandon ship, meaning that the loss of eleven men from one cargo ship was considered substantial.

Commander Graf and his U-69 were to go on to gain notoriety a few days later, on the night of October 14, when the ferry ss *Caribou* was torpedoed at Graf's command, with the loss of 136 lives.

## ss *Waterton*
*Torpedoed and sunk, October 14, 1942*

U-106, UNDER THE COMMAND OF HERMANN RASCH, entered the Cabot Strait under difficult conditions: air patrols spotted it constantly, forcing the captain to submerge and keeping the sub under constant pressure. By October 11, Rasch was running under the waves near St. Paul Island on the Cabot Strait where he sighted the convoy BS-31, on the Corner Brook–Sydney run. Only one escort ship could be seen, the armed yacht HMCS *Vision*. Rasch and his crew on U-106 picked the last merchant ship in the convoy, the British freighter SS *Waterton*. Rasch fired two torpedoes, both striking the *Waterton*. Though the cargo ship went down in nine minutes, all of the crew were rescued. Meanwhile, U-106 dove quickly and deeply to 185 metres, where it remained for eight hours, having been spotted and attacked by the HMCS *Vision*. It would be Rasch's last success in the Gulf area, even though he was able to penetrate up the St. Lawrence as far as Les Mechins. Air patrols made it too difficult for U-106, and it was forced to spend forty-two out of ninety-seven days of the mission submerged. Even the great Admiral Doenitz gave credit to Canadian air power, which was learning quickly how to work successfully with Canadian naval forces.

# CHAPTER FOUR

# CIVILIAN ENCOUNTERS WITH U-BOATS

FOR SIX LONG YEARS, CANADIAN NAVAL FORCES CLASHED with the formidable German U-boat menace. The conflict was constant, harrowing, and ever dangerous. Yet the Kriegsmarine, despite having its hands full with the ever-growing strength of the RCN, still made sure to try a variety of different tactics which it believed might just further its efforts. Several of these involved landing spies on Canadian soil, POW riots and classic escape attempts, sabotage, firing torpedoes at Canadian soil, and establishing a weather station on Canadian land. Other oddities included the loss of a U-boat due to a mishandled sewage flush, a respectful encounter with the *Bluenose*, a plan by the city of St. John's to burn to the ground rather than surrender it to the enemy, and the supposed capture of a U-boat in one of the Great Lakes.

## But First—Fact or Myth?

THROUGHOUT THE WAR, AND ESPECIALLY AFTER, STOR-ies have persisted of U-boat crews coming ashore in Newfoundland, Nova Scotia, New Brunswick, and Quebec. If these "urban legends" were accepted as fact, there would have been Germans milking cows in fields, eating lunch in restaurants, buying groceries, enjoying some cold ones in pubs, dancing with girls, and even going to movie theatres. Sometimes stories, told so many times over the years, become accepted as truth. People may have been observed in these places, perhaps speaking with a foreign accent, dressed a bit differently, and standing out in a crowd. But the fact is, no official documents support any of the above-mentioned events. Paranoia was rampant among the people of eastern Canada, especially those living along the coast, as U-boats were spotted just offshore. During the darkest days of the war, people truly expected a landing of some sort, especially those living in the Gaspé coast region.

## Encounter with the *Bluenose*

IN 1942 THE AGING *BLUENOSE* WAS SOLD TO TWO Americans and began its new career as a cargo vessel based out of Havana, Cuba. Sailing throughout the West Indies carrying anything from codfish to war munitions and aviation fuel, the schooner was marked as a fair target for enemy subs. On one memorable occasion, near Haiti, a U-boat did in fact surface within hailing distance of the *Bluenose*. This could easily have become tragic for the famed schooner and its crew, for at least two other sailing ships were sunk by German subs. But in this case the speedy schooner's fame saved it from disaster.

The U-boat commander recognized the famous *Bluenose* profile and hailed the captain to verify such. Indeed, the skipper replied, this truly is the famous *Bluenose*. The U-boat captain might have been a sailing enthusiast, for he answered, "If I didn't love that ship so, I would shell her right now," and sternly advised the skipper of the racing schooner to get back to Haiti at once, warning that if he came across them again he wouldn't be so generous. Surely fame, at times, does have its privileges.

## The *Mary Coady* Incident

DESPITE THE SOMETIMES HEAVY U-BOAT TRAFFIC OFF the shores of Newfoundland during the war, encounters with civilian fishing trawlers were rare. The *Mary Coady* encounter highlights the ingenuity and daring of U-boat captains when they had to take refuge in a hurry or be sunk.

On May 1, 1944, *U-548*, under Kapitänleutnant Heinrich Zimmermann, was spotted and attacked by a Liberator aircraft east of Conception Bay. Night was falling and so, under the cover of darkness, Zimmermann slipped away, surfacing two days later near Cape Broyle. *U-548*, quickly spotted by the British warship HMS *Hargood*, took refuge near some cliffs. The schooner *Mary Coady* entered the area and was quickly warned away from the search zone by the *Harwood*, whose captain ordered the schooner to spend the night at sea. The skipper of the small fishing boat, Tom Coady, wasn't about to argue and quickly left the area. About an hour later a crew member happened to glance overboard and notice a large shadow keeping pace with the schooner. There was no radio available aboard and no other way of signalling for help. So Captain Coady just nervously maintained his course, hoping the assumed U-boat would break off and seek protection away from the *Mary Coady*. By morning the crew noted, with no little relief, that the sub was gone. Safely underway once more, Zimmermann came across the HMCS *Valleyfield* two days later and hit it with an acoustic torpedo, sending the frigate to the bottom.

### *Flora Alberta* vs SS *Fanad Head*

THE *FLORA ALBERTA*, AT A MERE 93 TONS, WAS NO MATCH for a 3,000-ton, 420-foot cargo steamer such as the SS *Fanad Head*. But despite the war at sea, and despite convoys plowing through Newfoundland's U-boat-infested waters at all hours, Newfoundland fishers went on resolutely working the familiar waters, the only livelihood they knew. But the *Flora Alberta–Fanad Head* incident showed just how conditions such as heavy fog or violent weather can lead to tragedy in an instant.

On April 21, 1943, the *Flora Alberta*, out of Lunenburg, and its crew of twenty-seven men, under the command of Captain Gus Tanner, was in a heavy fog. Moving along the Nova Scotia coast near Halifax, Tanner kept the speed quite slow, at around four and a half knots, because the boat was nearing the fishing area. At the same time, the *Fanad Head* was approaching, leading the port column of an eight-ship convoy of cargo ships. The convoy was running at eight knots in blackout conditions and was blowing the fog whistle every ten minutes. At the last minute, the *Fanad Head* heard a fog signal from the *Flora Alberta*, but did not see the fishing vessel. A few minutes later the *Fanad Head* heard the *Flora Alberta*'s fog whistle once more, but it was much too late to take effective evasive action, as the *Flora Alberta* appeared out of the mist directly in front of the *Fanad Head*. A collision was unavoidable and the cargo ship sliced into the fishing vessel, cutting it clean in two.

The *Flora Alberta* went down so quickly that only seven of her crew could be rescued. A subsequent inquiry attached a degree of blame to both ships, but the whole tragic incident must be accepted for what it really was: a casualty of the naval war being fought in great part in the front yards of Newfoundland, and of Canada.

## U-boat Attack on the
## Wabana (Bell Island) Anchorage

NEWFOUNDLAND, NOT YET A CANADIAN PROVINCE IN 1942, was especially vulnerable to German attacks since the island territory lay directly in the path of Allied shipping. U-boats patrolled the area heavily, searching for targets.

The mines of Bell Island, in Conception Bay, supplied the steel mills of Cape Breton with much-needed iron ore. The Germans knew that the Sydney mills supplied nearly one-third of Canada's steel production and that a successful attack could seriously hamper Allied output. It would take a dangerous and daring raid to successfully pull off such a coup, but German U-boats took up the challenge.

In early September 1942, U-513, commanded by Rolf Ruggeberg, decided to move in closer to St. John's after patrolling further out near the Strait of Belle Isle with little action. On September 4, spotting the small ore carrier *Evelyn B* heading to Conception Bay, Ruggeberg decided to follow.

Passing through the anchorage under the cover of darkness, and despite the presence of several shore batteries, U-513 settled in the bottom at twenty-four metres, waiting to see what the morning would bring. Easy pickings, as it turned out. Ruggeberg spotted several cargo ships at anchor. The SS

*Strathcona* and SS *Saganaga* were targeted, going down with a loss of twenty-nine men, all from the latter. Incredibly, in broad daylight and under the guns of shore batteries, U-513 made a successful surface getaway, shocking area residents greatly. Many believed that if the Germans could make such a raid so easily, they might very well attempt a major shore landing.

But the German subs were not yet finished with Bell Island. Friedrich Wissmann, commander of U-513's sister ship, U-518, was not about to let Ruggeberg get all the glory and, on November 2, decided to stage his own attack. Moving up into Conception Bay, Wissmann waited. Despite the increased

*The merchant carrier* Rose Castle, *torpedoed by a U-boat on November 2, 1942, near Bell Island, Newfoundland. Despite shore batteries and a corvette presence,* U-518, *daring as usual, slipped into the anchorage, causing tremendous destruction and confusion before slipping away into the darkness.* (Library and Archives Canada PA-143173)

shore vigilance, roving shore lights, and the presence of a corvette and several fairmile patrol boats, U-518 was able to enter the anchorage. A short time later, Wissmann selected the SS *Anna T* as its prime target. The torpedo missed and continued on to detonate at the loading dock. The ensuing blast woke just about everyone at Bell Island, causing fear and consternation among the residents of the community. Pandemonium followed as yet another blast erupted. Ruggeberg was not finished yet and fired two more torpedoes at the SS *Rose Castle*, which went down quickly and lost twenty-eight of its crew. The PLM-27 was the next to go, along with twelve of its crew. Taking advantage of the mass confusion which followed, U-518 made a successful escape.

These attacks on ships resting at the dock would have caused as much mayhem and confusion as a land attack for the people who lived practically at dockside. This, along with

*Torpedo damage at Scotia Pier following U-518's brazen attack on Bell Island, November 2, 1942. The local citizenry was shocked and fearful that the Germans might attempt a shore landing.* (Library and Archives Canada PA-188854)

the terrible loss of the ferry *Caribou* shook the townspeople greatly. The enemy was virtually on their doorstep, and the people of Newfoundland could hardly deny that, despite being four thousand kilometres from Europe, they were now on the front lines of a great and terrible conflict.

## Torpedo Beaches at St. Yvon, Gaspé

THE BELL ISLAND ATTACK RESULTED IN THE ONLY TORPEDO to explode on Newfoundland soil, but it was not the only torpedo to come ashore. The small village of St. Yvon on the

*Gaspé Bay near Ships Head where U-boat torpedoes came ashore. Residents along the Gaspé shore on the St. Lawrence River often watched helplessly as both merchant and RCN ships were attacked by U-boats. In this case, the torpedo missed its target and came ashore but did not detonate. It was kept for years by a local citizen.* (Library and Archives Canada E010861899)

northern Gaspé shore in Quebec also experienced the firing of a German torpedo. On September 8, 1942, U-165, patrolling the area and always alert for a fresh kill, spotted the SS *Meadcliffe Hall* and fired a single torpedo. It missed. The torpedo continued on and spent itself on the local beach directly in front of the rock cliffs of the tiny seaside village of St. Yvon. Still mostly intact, the torpedo was picked up and turned over to the military by local resident Roch Coté. Eventually it was returned to Coté, who, along with his family, proudly exhibited the ordnance for years until it was finally taken over by the Musée de la Gaspésie and subsequently restored by the Centre de Conservation du Québec. Needless to say, the residents of St. Yvon were proud of their unique artefact, especially since it was personally delivered to their tiny community.

## The Impossible Journey

MANY PEOPLE STILL BELIEVE THAT U-505, NOW AT THE Museum of Science and Industry in Chicago, was, in fact, captured in one of the Great Lakes during the Second World War. As the story goes, the sub commander thought he could just slip into the Great Lakes and get some easy tonnage, apparently unaware of the lock system and its usage.

In reality, U-505 had a successful, albeit short, career, taking part in twelve war patrols until its capture off West Africa in 1944. The sub was later taken to the United States and in 1954 was put on display as a museum ship in Chicago. This was an easy myth to perpetuate, however, as many museum visitors could not figure out how the sub could have "sailed" so far inland.

## Sewer Sinks Sub

TO BE SUNK DUE TO A MALFUNCTIONING TOILET SEEMS A rather inglorious way for a U-boat's career to end, given their reputation as such high-tech pieces of equipment, but it was as simple as opening the wrong valve. In this case, the captain couldn't blame any of his crew, as it was he himself who mishandled the flush, leading to disaster.

It happened eight days into the first patrol of U-1206, under the command of Karl Schlitt. Schlitt needed to answer a call of nature and was having difficulty managing the valve flush system. Too embarrassed to call out for some crew member who had training in the high pressure flush system, Schlitt instead tried to figure out the works himself. The captain only managed to spray everything around him with seawater— and worse, raw sewage! By the time he, with help, managed to stop the water flow, the toilet floor was flooded. Much of the water leaked through the floor into the room below. That room, unfortunately, held the ship's batteries. The battery acid quickly reacted to the seawater, forming extremely toxic chlorine gas. Kapitan Schlitt had no choice but to surface immediately. Everything would have been okay once on the surface. It was just a matter of venting the air and cleaning up a bit. But U-1206, only sixteen kilometres off Peterhead in the North Sea, was quickly spotted by British patrol planes and attacked. The totally discouraged and disgusted Schlitt surrendered after scuttling his own ship. Makes one wonder what Kapitan Schlitt did for the previous eight days without obvious use of the toilet.

## Armed Landing in Labrador

DESPITE THE CLOSE PROXIMITY OF U-BOATS TO THE eastern Canadian shoreline, there has only been one verified account of an armed excursion on North American soil during the Second World War. It happened in October 1943, and was kept secret until details were found in a logbook among Second World War archives in Frieberg, Germany, in the late 1970s.

The Germans were always interested in weather patterns and formations in the Northern Hemisphere because of the west-to-east movements. West European countries, including Germany, relied on approaching Atlantic weather patterns to schedule military operations for their ground, air, and naval forces. Without proper data, accurate weather forecasting was very difficult. To this end, German ships, U-boats, and planes, all specially equipped to gather meteorological data, were sent throughout the North Atlantic. But these mobile weather stations were highly susceptible to Allied attack or capture. Some sort of semi-permanent weather station on solid ground was needed. The Germans found a solution with the development of an automatic, battery-generated weather station. It contained a Lorenz FK-type transmitter, anemometer, wind vane, and several canisters containing nickel-cadmium batteries which could power the Wetter-Funkgerät Land-26 weather station, as it was called, for up to six months.

In 1943 it was decided to deploy one of these portable weather stations to the coast of northern Labrador. U-537, under Kapitänleutnant Peter Schrewe, was assigned to carry out this task. On board the sub was German scientist Dr. Kurt Sommermeyer, who would head up the project, which was code-named Weather Station Kurt. After encountering terrible storm conditions on the way over, U-537 arrived in

Martin Bay in northern Labrador on October 22, 1943, found a remote and safe spot, and waited for the anticipated fog, which soon set in. While part of the crew affected repairs to the storm-damaged sub, Dr. Sommermeyer, his assistant, and a dozen or so crew members were detailed to ferry the ten large canisters ashore and up to a hilltop approximately 350 metres inland. Several others were positioned as lookouts, presumably armed. To divert suspicion if discovered, equipment was labelled *Property of the Canadian Meteor Service*, which didn't exist, even though the area was part of the Dominion of Newfoundland and not yet a Canadian province. The Germans also scattered empty American cigarette packages around the site.

For the next twenty-nine hours, Sommermeyer and the U-boat's crew worked to set up the station properly and to repair the damaged sub. After ensuring the weather station was working properly and that the U-boat was fixed, they were good to go. Seventy days later, after surviving three attacks by Allied aircraft, *U-573* finally reached its home port of Lorient, France. The sub was eventually transferred to the Far East where, in late 1944, it was sunk with the loss of all on board. Only Dr. Sommermeyer and one crew member of *U-573*, who were not aboard when the boat was lost, survived the war.

Transmission reports indicate that the weather station lasted for only a couple of days before stopping completely and inexplicably. No reports indicate frequency jamming, so the weather station lay useless, forgotten except for a handful of crew members and of course Dr. Sommermeyer. The event came to life once more in the mid-seventies when a retired German engineer decided to research and write a book on the German Weather Service and came across Sommermeyer's papers as well as a photograph of the weather site and a picture of a sub at anchor, purported to be *U-573*, at Martin Bay.

In 1981 the Canadian Coast Guard found the remnants of Weather Station Kurt. The artefacts can now be viewed at the Canadian War Museum at Ottawa. The Kurt project, which proved to be the only armed landing on North American soil in the Second World War, nearly became the first of two armed landings. In 1944, U-867 set out to install a second weather station, also in Labrador, but was attacked and sunk by Allied planes before it could arrive.

## The Reluctant Spy

AFTER THE US ENTERED THE WAR IN 1941, HITLER DECIDED to land secret agents on American and Canadian soil, hoping to learn more about Allied shipping, installations, and any other information which might help the German war effort. However, the whole scheme did not work out too well, as all spies were discovered and at least six, captured in the US, were executed.

Alfred Langbein lived and worked over five years in Canada before returning home to his native Germany just as Hitler was taking over the reins of power. Within a few years, Langbein was recruited by the Abwehr, the intelligence arm of the Nazi regime. There he was trained in espionage and sabotage techniques. After a few assignments, which did not turn out as planned, or were cancelled, the Abwehr came up with a new plan to land in North America. It was to be a U-boat drop in Canada. Langbein was to be put ashore at a remote area, bury his gear, then make his way to major ports of Halifax or Montreal, hopefully blending in the communities for a few months, then return and retrieve his buried radio. He would then send in nightly radio reports on any important information he could gather. If his radio were broken he was to send regular letters written in invisible ink to mail drops in Switzerland.

Langbein boarded U-213 on April 25, 1943. While most of the crossing was tedious, there was one incident off Portugal, when U-213 was attacked by a destroyer, forcing the sub to crash dive to 200 metres as depth charges detonated around the boat. The U-boat escaped, the crew shaken considerably but unscathed. By May 12, the sub surfaced near the tiny fishing village of St. Martins in southern New Brunswick. A small dinghy was quickly made ready for Langbein and his gear. An officer and two crew members brought the loaded dinghy safely to shore and helped Langbein drag and carry his equipment across the rock-strewn beach and up a steep 80-metre hill.

Several hours later the dinghy and crew, who were led to believe that Langbein was spying for the elite German Propaganda Kompany, were back aboard U-213 ready to depart, leaving the newly landed spy to his own devices.

After sleeping for a few hours, Langbein made his way through rough terrain to St. Martins, where he managed to clean up a bit before hitching a ride on a lumber truck heading to Saint John. The spy could speak English, but with a heavy German accent, so it was just a matter of pretending to be hoarse from a cold to disguise his voice. Within a few days Langbein found himself in Montreal, a city he knew quite well. In fact, he checked into the same boarding house he'd stayed in ten years before.

Now, Langbein was not lacking funds for his great spy adventure. His superiors supplied him with $7,500, all in US $50 bills, often making it difficult to use. By June 17, 1942, Langbein found himself enjoying a cold beer in a Montreal bordello when Montreal's finest raided the place. Although his only form of identification was an employment card and his German accent was quite strong, he was let go with a $50 fine. Now a little nervous, the spy decided to get out of Dodge and quickly booked a train ticket to Ottawa.

On arriving he settled in at the Grand Hotel on Sussex, which was, at that time, a favourite watering hole for military personnel, politicians, and journalists. It was, in fact, the perfect place for a spy to set up shop. For a year, despite his German accent and abundance of $50 bills, Langbein built a large circle of friends, many of whom were in the military. Several of his acquaintances were secretaries working for Naval Intelligence.

Langbein would be hard-pressed to find a better prompt to get to work as a spy. But the truth was, he was enjoying himself far too much to put himself at risk with clandestine activities. He wasn't worried about the Abwehr. Instead Langbein, with his friends, took in parties, picnics, sports events, and excursions, often picking up the tab. On one occasion, he was taken on a tour of top-secret naval intelligence experimental farm, undoubtedly a spy's dream. Still, no questions, no suspicion, or threatening interest directed towards Langbein. He felt the best way to avoid suspicion was not to do anything suspicious. It worked out pretty well. Only on one occasion was he confronted and accused of being a spy, by a drunken soldier who wasn't at all taken seriously by the authorities. Still, Langbein was shaken by this close call and moved out of the Grand Hotel into lodgings in Lowertown, taking a room with a family who thought he was Dutch. Although still spending lavishly, Langbein was becoming worried as his money dwindled. It didn't help that he had stashed $2,000 in a bottle and buried it but could not remember exactly where.

Finally, on November 2, 1944, Langbein decided to turn himself in. Not an easy decision, since he preferred not to be shot as a spy, which, technically, he was not: not once had he make any contact with Germany during his period in Canada. He was interrogated extensively, especially about the Enigma decoder he may have had access to on the way over. Langbein insisted that he had no interest or intention of spying for the Abwehr and had planned to turn himself in months before. In the end, Langbein's life was spared, and he spent the rest of the war in an internment camp. He was found not guilty of spying because he had not committed any true acts of sabotage against Canada during the war. Released at the end of the conflict, Langbein, who, it seems, simply wanted to enjoy life in Canada for a bit, rejoined his wife and family in Germany.

## What was the Abwehr thinking?

ON NOVEMBER 9, 1942, THE ABWEHR PUT ASHORE another agent, this time at New Carlisle, a village located on the Bay of Chaleur's Gaspé coast. Werner Alfred Waldemar von Janowski, an officer in the German Kriegsmarine, was trained as a German agent, but as a spy, Janowski was a complete bust—especially at avoiding detection. Janowski travelled to his drop-off courtesy of U-518, and like his predecessor Langbein, found himself under enemy attack after U-518 pulled off a daring raid and getaway on the Bell Island, Newfoundland, installations. When U-518 finally arrived at its destination forty-four days later, Janowski was ready. Or at least he thought he was. Perhaps, with some arrogance, he believed the people of Gaspé to be mere local yokels who would never suspect a spy in their midst. He was proven, in a short time, quite wrong in his assessment.

At around 0400 hours, Janowski arrived by dinghy on shore, about six kilometres from New Carlisle. After burying his naval uniform, he set out by foot to catch the train from New Carlisle to Montreal. If caught he planned to claim to be a deserter and would demand to be taken as a prisoner of war. The two heavy bags he carried with him contained his powerful transmitter as well as a large array of equipment, all tools of the espionage trade. After waiting for daylight, Janowski started walking the six kilometres to the small village, accepting a ride at one point by a local CNR employee. Checking in at a hotel, he asked for a room with a bath.

The hotel manager, Earle Annett, immediately noticed several inconsistencies. The stranger spoke with a guttural French accent, though he called himself William Branton from Toronto. The man also stunk to high heaven, some kind of oil or diesel smell. His clothing, dishevelled as they were, had a distinct European styling. Now, Mr. Branton said he had just gotten off the bus outside of the village and walked into town, but Annett knew there were no buses scheduled at that early hour. In fact, the bus was not scheduled to arrive until noon. And there was more. Janowski paid for his room with two Canadian dollar bills, which had not been in circulation for years. And the matches he used to light his cigarette were marked *Fabrique en Belgique* (made in Belgium); his cigarettes were also Belgian made. Annett offered Janowski a lift to the train station to catch the 11:10 train, but the spy refused this offer and set out by foot.

As soon as Janowski left, the suspicious hotel manager decided to contact Constable Alphonse Duchesneau of the Quebec Provincial Police. Duchesneau jumped aboard the train just as it was pulling away from the station, found his man, and politely began asking a series of tough questions. Finally the QPP officer asked Janowski, who was looking ever more suspicious, to open his luggage. Janowski now knew the gig was up, and declared, "I am a German officer and I serve my country just as you do." The train stopped at the next station, Bonaventure, where a patrol car was waiting to take Janowski back to New Carlisle.

Now in custody, Janowski attempted to use his "prisoner of war" plan. He was permitted to wear his uniform and hat, but kept his civilian pants. Janowski was later "turned" as a double agent, and was handled by the RCMP for eighteen months before being turned over to the British. However, this scheme resulted in mixed success since he never returned or completed many of the communiqués with the British. As to U-518, it met its fate during an Allied counterattack in the mid-Atlantic on April 22, 1945, when it was destroyed and sunk by Hedgehog depth charges. All aboard were lost.

The Janowski affair seems to be just the opposite of Langbein: while the latter had more than a few opportunities to set up a major espionage base in Canada, the former was foolishly unprepared. In fact, the Janowski attempt was so inept, many in high espionage circles reasoned that he was possibly set up by the Abwehr to be captured, where he could then be used as a triple agent.

## Operation Kiebitz vs Operation Pointe Maisonette

DURING THE SECOND WORLD WAR, THE GERMAN MINISTRY of Propaganda was always on the alert for further opportunities to extol the virtues of their fighting forces; this helped bolster morale where needed and showed the German people how brave and dedicated these young men were.

The Kriegsmarine controlled a very adept and powerful U-boat fleet, under the able command of the much respected Admiral Karl Doenitz. Doenitz, having years of experience as a submarine commander, knew full well the terrible conditions the fifty or so men on each boat would face during a patrol, some lasting up to three months. Due to the conditions and dangers faced, ships left their home docks amid great fanfare.

On returning, if they did, crewmen were welcomed as true heroes and given the best treatment possible. Lodging, food and drinks, first-class transportation to family homes, media coverage, and medals—lots of medals—were lavished upon the returning crew members.

Despite the initial success of Doenitz's U-boats against Allied merchant ships, many German subs were lost or captured, and for survivors it was off to a prisoner of war (POW) camp until war's end. A POW camp had been established in Bowmanville, Ontario, located about 80 kilometres from Toronto. Many of those incarcerated at Bowmanville were high-echelon officers and others with skills and knowledge advantageous to the RCN. But Bowmanville, situated 1,500 kilometres from the Atlantic shores, was considered a secure location. Escape was believed to be unrealistic and unlikely. Besides, most inmates reported that conditions at Bowmanville were quite acceptable and many prisoners were, in fact, in no hurry to leave.

Several of the POWs at Bowmanville, especially those decorated with honours for loyal service, felt that it was their duty to attempt to escape. Among those enjoying the hospitality of Bowmanville was a group of submarine officers including the top U-boat ace Otto Kretchmer, known as the "Atlantic Wolf." Others included Kapitänleutnant Hans Ey, Joachim von Knebel-Doberitz, Wolfgang Heyda, and Horst Elfe, one of Doenitz's favourites. In the fall of 1942, Kretchmer, undoubtedly longing to get back to a periscope, devised an elaborate escape plan involving several tunnels to freedom. Three tunnels were started at once. If one or two were discovered, the third would be used. On reaching freedom outside the walls, the escapees would make their way to the little town of Bathurst, New Brunswick. From there it was three to four days' walk to a secluded point of land and cove called Pointe de Maisonnette. At this location a German U-boat would be waiting just off shore, ready to send in a small dinghy to shuttle the escapees to freedom.

In theory, it was a fairly good plan and Kretchmer was able to convince his boss, Doenitz, that the strategy was indeed workable. After reading all the escape details in a coded letter from Kretchmer, Doenitz, thinking of the enormous propaganda benefits the escape would generate, approved the daring plan. Further encoded communication indicated Doenitz was sending U-536, which would be off Pointe de Maisonnette from September 23 to October 7, waiting for the escaping officers to arrive and signal to be picked up. A torrent of encoded messages was sent between Bowmanville and Germany giving full details of their plans. Obviously a lot of confidence was put into the Enigma encoders. Unfortunately for the Germans, the Canadian Military Intelligence and the RCMP were active and quite successful in decoding all messages concerning the breakout, and more.

The tunnelling went ahead as scheduled, some men taking turns on a round-the-clock-shift basis while others worked on false documents, identification papers, clothing, travelling goods, etc. Everything went along smoothly until a week before the escape date, when the second floor of a prison building suddenly collapsed under the weight of—you guessed it—tunnelled earth! Two of the three escape routes were quickly discovered. The frustrated Kretchmer could wait no longer and decided they would make their move the next night, using the third tunnel. The luck of the would-be escapees got worse on the following day, when the third, and last, tunnel collapsed into a hole right next to the prison fence. Four months of digging wasted! (The RCMP, who were monitoring the tunnelling progress all along, had planned to pick up the prisoners as they emerged from the tunnels.)

As Kretchmer's plans evaporated, another prisoner stepped forward with a daring plan of his own. Käpitanleutnant Wolfgang Heyda, the incarcerated commander of U-434, had put together a brave plan, though foolhardy and somewhat reckless. But Kretchmer listened.

Heyda would use a bosun's chair attached to the camp's electricity cables. Using the chair, he would slide down over the walls and barbed wire, and away to Pointe de Maisonnette and freedom. The danger of being electrocuted by the hi-voltage wires or simply getting shot was shrugged off by the audacious Heyda, who, Kretchmer decided, would be their man.

Thus began, on a cool September evening in 1943, part II of the Great Escape, Bowmanville style. Heyda donned his gear, including civilian clothing, documents, and money. Boots with nails driven through the soles served as crampons as Heyda scurried up a pole attached to a power line high over the compound fence. Quickly securing his bosun's chair to the power cable running over the prison fence, Heyda was off. Landing on the outside of the camp fence without detection, he was on his way.

Travelling by CNR train and able to converse in near flawless English, Heyda found himself in Bathurst, New Brunswick, without incident by September 26. So far so good. It was now a mere eighty kilometres to the rendezvous at the Pointe de Maisonnette lighthouse. At one point of his hike he was challenged by a war patrol, but was saved by his papers, clothing, and quick thinking. That same evening Heyda arrived at his destination, or almost. Stopped on the Maisonnette beach, he was once again released. A short time later, however, he was picked up by sentries and brought to the lighthouse where he was questioned by Desmond Piers. Piers headed up the land control of Operation Pointe Maisonnette, which included two radar units, a platoon of combat engineers, forty men of the

Royal Canadian Artillery, at least two-dozen drivers of the Army Service Corps, and a section of combat engineers. This was all in preparation for the plan to capture or destroy the German submarine they knew to be in the vicinity of Pointe de Maisonnette.

As planned, *U-536*, under Kapitänleutnant Rolf Schauenberg, had reached its rendezvous point on September 26 and was waiting for the signal from the escaped prisoners. Schauenberg did not know of the failed tunnel attempts or of Heyda's escape. And, like the rest of the German Naval High Command, Schauenberg and Heyda did not realize that the Canadian Intelligence Services and the RCMP had decoded all communications regarding the escape and rendezvous and had carefully set a trap for the wary, but as yet unsuspecting, sub. Heyda was returned to Bowmanville. Lieutenant Piers felt slightly averse to this, as it meant that Heyda's superiors would soon learn that Canadian intelligence could decode German messages. A major anti-sub attack force of over a dozen warships, headed by the HMCS *Rimouski* and well aware of *U-536*'s presence, was hidden just behind Caraquet Island waiting for the signal to pounce. It was a well-planned affair which suited the RCN, but German submarine commanders were well-known for getting out of tight spots. The looming, unseen, and unknown threat would soon prove to be formidable indeed for Schauenberg and his crew.

Meanwhile, Schauenberg signalled at several prearranged times, but received no response. He was getting a bit nervous and more than a little suspicious. Lieutenant Piers, knowing a quick, successful capture might come down to the next few moments, decided to have a signal sent which said "Komm, komm," meaning "come in, come in." Schauenberg at once realized that this was not the proper message and, in addition, it had not been sent on the agreed-upon frequency. Moving back to deeper water, the U-536 commander ordered a crash dive just as the *Rimouski* and several other warships sped frantically to the U-boat's position. The chase was on. For most of the night, Schauenberg kept his boat on the bottom; while it was rocked continuously by depth charges, it managed to avoid serious damage. The next morning the sub moved to deeper water, still avoiding a direct hit.

But a submarine crew cannot survive being submerged for more than twenty-four to forty-eight hours. Shauenberg's men were passing out from lack of oxygen and he knew he would have to surface or all would perish. Surfacing at dawn following the night-long attack, U-536 found the sea quiet with no ships in sight, giving the sub a chance to recharge its batteries. Later that day the sub became entangled in a trawler's fishing net which had wrapped around the U-boat's conning tower. Finally the desperate sub managed to leave the area as the attack ships concentrated on a different zone of the Bay of Chaleur. Kapitänleutnant Schauenberg could not get out of the area fast enough, saying later:

> *The experience in Chaleur Bay had severely tested us. I had only one objective: finding a quiet area 600 miles south, that is to say, far from the enemy's operational flying zone. We urgently needed to surface to allow the men to recover and to make repairs.*

So, both Operation Kiebitz and its counterpart Operation Pointe Maisonnette have to be deemed failures. U-536 was later destroyed in November 1943, in the North Atlantic by the British frigate HMS *Nene*. Heyda was eventually released in 1947 and returned to Germany. He died of polio at Kiel, a mere three months after his release.

# SOURCES

Bercuson, David, and Holger H. Herwig. *Deadly Seas: The Duel Between the St. Croix and the U305 in the Battle of the Atlantic.* Toronto: Random House, 1997.

Douglas, W. A. B. *No Higher Purpose: The Official Operational History of the Royal Canadian Navy in the Second World War.* St. Catherines, ON: Vanwell Publishing, 2002.

Dunmore, Spencer. *In Great Waters: The Epic Story of the Battle of the Atlantic, 1939–45.* Toronto: McClelland and Stewart, 2000.

Hadley, Michael L. *U-boats Against Canada: German Submarines in Canadian Waters.* Kingston: McGill-Queen's, 1990.

Juno Beach Centre: www.junobeach.org

Milner, Marc. "The Humble Corvette: Navy, Part 27." *Legion Magazine.* June 5, 2008.

———. *Battle of the Atlantic.* Stroud, ON: Tempus, 2005.

———. *The U-boat Hunters: The Royal Canadian Navy and the Offensive Against Germany's Submarines, 1943–1945.* Toronto: University of Toronto Press, 1994.

———. *North Atlantic Run: The Royal Canadian Navy and the Battle for the Convoys.* Markham, ON: Penguin, 1990.

Macpherson, Ken. *Corvettes of the Royal Canadian Navy 1939–1945.* St. Catherines, ON: Vanwell, 2000.

Naval Museum of Manioba. "Roll Call of Ships Lost at Sea, 1939–1945." www.naval-museum.mb.ca/ships/rollcall.htm

Newfoundland and Labrador Heritage: www.heritage.nf.ca/

U-boat.net: www.uboat.net

Williamson, Gordon. *Wolf Pack: The Story of the U-boat in WWII.* Oxford: Osprey Publishing, 2005.

# INDEX

# Index